Julie Hiram... ...of Virtue have been h...p...g ...aracter in their children for years now. *Guardians of Purity* combines common sense and biblical wisdom to help parents guide their kids through the choppy waters of our sex-saturated culture.

—JIM DALY
PRESIDENT, FOCUS ON THE FAMILY

Bravo, Julie! This book is a much-needed tool that concerned and diligent parents everywhere will greatly appreciate! For nearly two decades I have spoken to young people about purity. In that time I have met countless parents who are craving the wisdom and encouragement that this book provides about that very subject. Blessings to you in your ministry, Julie—keep up the great work!

—REBECCA ST. JAMES
SINGER, AUTHOR, ACTRESS

Julie Hiramine is one of my favorite voices in the Purity Revolution that's rising up around the world, and her commitment to that cause is straight and true. I've ministered to many people at her side, from the mountains of Vail to the islands of Indonesia, and I know her husband, Kay, and her wonderful five children. She walks the talk and takes on that parental role as the guardian of purity in her home seriously. On that basis alone she's earned the right to be heard, so listen up and listen well. The enemy wants your kids, but you can keep them safe.

—FRED STOEKER
COAUTHOR OF *EVERY MAN'S BATTLE*, *PREPARING YOUR SON FOR EVERY MAN'S BATTLE*, AND *HERO*

Julie's book *Guardians of Purity* is an amazing resource filled with crucial information and wisdom from above. This should be in the "must read" category for every parent.

—RICK JOYNER
FOUNDER AND EXECUTIVE DIRECTOR OF
MORNINGSTAR MINISTRIES

Julie Hiramine's *Guardians of Purity* carries her life's work and passion, which is to help the next generation make the wise choices that will best set them up for a lifetime of healthy, happy relationships. Your student's heart is in loving wise hands with Julie's wisdom.

—PAM FARREL
AUTHOR OF *THE 10 BEST DECISIONS A PARENT CAN MAKE, GOT TEENS?*, AND *RAISING A MODERN-DAY PRINCESS*

Julie Hiramine has gifted parents trying to navigate the many distracting and often destructive land mines of our culture with a practical guide for raising confident and Christ-honoring kids. With her heart engaged and her hand on the pulse of today's trends and technology, her informative book will inspire you. You'll no longer just desire to see your children transform into godly young adults; you'll also be empowered with the tools to help them do so.

—KAREN EHMAN
PROVERBS 31 MINISTRIES NATIONAL DIRECTOR
OF SPEAKERS, AUTHOR

*Guardians of Purity* is a book that all parents should own, read, and allow to change their lives. Convicting, inspiring, informative, this book reveals the reality of the moral dilemma for children in this generation. Julie is a powerful and passionate voice, anointed by God, calling parents and youth to live out and to understand the powerful significance of moral purity in their personal lives. Julie clearly communicates that if we are to be holy and set apart for God's purposes, we must be holy in our conduct, and we must take responsibility for the moral and spiritual health of our families and children. Please read this book, and buy a copy for every parent that you know!

—SALLY CLARKSON
DIRECTOR OF WHOLE HEART MINISTRIES,
AUTHOR, CONFERENCE SPEAKER

Julie Hiramine recognizes the overwhelming need for parents to be deeply involved in the lives of their children, especially starting at a young age. With so many things in society targeting their moral values, this is a resource you can't afford to miss.

—RON AND LYNETTE LEWIS
PASTORS, AUTHORS, FOUNDERS OF
STOPCHILDTRAFFICKINGNOW.ORG

As a police officer and father of six children I work to keep my finger on the pulse of today's culture and how it's impacting my family. In *Guardians of Purity* Julie Hiramine delivers a hard-hitting perspective on both the traditional struggles facing our families and the ever-growing unique battle for the heart and mind of every child. Julie not only creates an urgency to jump into the trenches with our kids, but she also equips us in powerful ways to lead them on a journey of hope.

—JON HOLSTEN
CHILD SAFETY ADVOCATE, POLICE SERGEANT,
AUTHOR OF *THE SWIMSUIT LESSON*

Julie's book provides a clear message of hope to all parents. She makes it clear that we don't need to wish for the "good old days" of purity for young people. Instead she shows ways for us to strategically plan to make purity part of young life in *today's generation*.

—BRIAN D. MOLITOR
FOUNDER, MALACHI GLOBAL FOUNDATION

In today's "anything-goes-morality" culture there are few voices that champion the cause of moral purity. Julie Hiramine is one of those voices. And it is one thing to raise a voice on a purely biblio-philosphical level and quite another to provide real, practical, commonsense advice. What you hold in your hands is tried and true, practical, hands-on advice about how parents can equip their children to live a life of moral purity.

—MICHAEL FLETCHER
SENIOR PASTOR

Well, finally someone has put it all together. Julie Hiramine not only identifies the issues that parents and teens are confronting, but she also gives practical guidance on how to deal with the myriad challenges associated with raising children or with just being a teenager today. This mother of five is speaking from experience and not theory. This book is the best on the market for parents who need some workable solutions to raising and mentoring children and guiding them to a life of purity and obedience to God. Thanks, Julie. This is a real blessing.

—LTG (RET.) WILLIAM G. BOYKIN
FOUNDER OF KINGDOM WARRIORS MINISTRIES,
AUTHOR OF *NEVER SURRENDER* AND
*DANGER CLOSE*

It's tempting as parents to feel outmanned by what seems like an omnipresent assault on the purity of our children, but as Julie Hiramine demonstrates in this book, there is real hope if we are aware, active, and vigilant. The best part of this book is that it offers what parents need most: practical, real-life strategies. The strategies not only will help students understand their value as image-bearers and the importance of purity, but they will also help parents create opportunities for practice in important life-shaping habits of virtue.

—JOHN STONESTREET
SUMMIT MINISTRIES, THE CHUCK COLSON
CENTER FOR CHRISTIAN WORLDVIEW

Julie Hiramine has written a book that all parents should read, whether their children are toddlers or young adults. This book is a thoughtful road map through the confusing terrain of sexuality. *Guardians of Purity* will encourage you that so much *more* is possible for this generation, and it will guide you with easy-to-implement ideas to impact your children to make life-giving choices about their sexuality.

—SHARON A. HERSH, MA, LPC
AUTHOR OF *MOM, SEX IS NO BIG DEAL* AND
*MOM, I FEEL FAT*

Julie Hiramine's new book, *Guardians of Purity*, is a refreshing must-read for every parent and pastor concerned about training godly children in our generation. This book will encourage and assist any parent committed to raising children to live in purity and obedience to the Lord. *Guardians of Purity* is biblically based and extremely practical. It offers realistic ideas and suggestions that can be applied immediately. Julie pulls no punches; she tells it like it is. Thank you, Julie, for this major contribution to the families of our generation.

—LARRY AND LAVERNE KREIDER
INTERNATIONAL DIRECTOR OF DOVE
INTERNATIONAL, AUTHORS

Too often we hear statistics with few hints for how to deal with the problems they describe. Julie Hiramine not only successfully encapsulates the challenges every Christian parent faces in today's world, but she also skillfully allows readers to plug in their own details and create deliberate strategies for successfully parenting their children in the area of purity. Julie shows moms and dads how to recognize, mentor, deal with, and create teaching tools to address the unique bents in their kids from infancy on. This book is destined to become a valuable resource for parents everywhere interested in raising a spiritually, physically, and emotionally pure generation of sons and daughters.

—LYNDA HUNTER BJORKLUND, EdD
FOUNDER OF CREATED FOR PURPOSE,
AUTHOR, SPEAKER

# GUARDIANS OF PURITY

### A PARENT'S GUIDE TO WINNING THE WAR AGAINST MEDIA, PEER PRESSURE, AND ERODING SEXUAL VALUES

# JULIE HIRAMINE

CHARISMA
HOUSE

GUARDIANS OF PURITY by Julie Hiramine
Published by Charisma House
Charisma Media/Charisma House Book Group
600 Rinehart Road
Lake Mary, Florida 32746
www.charismahouse.com

Copyright © 2012 by Julie Hiramine
All rights reserved

Cover design by Rachel Lopez
Design Director: Bill Johnson

Visit the author's website at www.generationsofvirtue.org.

Library of Congress Cataloging-in-Publication Data:
An application to register this book for cataloging has been submitted to the Library of Congress.
International Standard Book Number: 978-1-61638-855-3
E-book ISBN: 978-1-61638-856-0

While the author has made every effort to provide accurate telephone numbers and Internet addresses at the time of publication, neither the publisher nor the author assumes any responsibility for errors or for changes that occur after publication.

First edition

12 13 14 15 16 — 9 8 7 6 5 4 3 2 1
Printed in the United States of America

*To Kay, my husband.*

*May God continue to knit
our hearts to raise up the next
generation together.*

Pure and genuine religion in the sight of
God the Father means caring for orphans
and widows in their distress and refusing
to let the world corrupt you.

—JAMES 1:27, NLT

# CONTENTS

# ACKNOWLEDGMENTS

Thank you to the Generations of Virtue team.
Your countless hours of volunteer ministry make
you dear to God's heart.

Thank you to Mary, who has been my mentor,
confidante, and friend.

I am grateful also to my family; as I have written
this book, you are the generation
God has called to carry His standard
to future generations.
Thank you for all your support!
This would have not been possible without you.

Introduction

# WAKE UP AND SMELL THE DECEPTION

IT'S INSIDIOUS. IT'S subtle. The world that revolves around our kids' lives is incrementally inching into their hearts and minds, shaping and molding them into a replica of its values, trends, and worldviews. This tsunami that breaks down the doors of our homes and crashes on the living room floor has an impact that is far-reaching. Take a look at what this world brings to the dinner table for our kids to feast upon:

🔒 A sexual scene occurs on TV 6.7 times per hour.[1]

- The average teen spends one hour forty minutes per week browsing for pornography.[2]

- One of our every three females in the United States gets pregnant before the age of twenty.[3]

- Approximately 65 percent of graduating high school seniors have had sexual intercourse.[4]

- Seventy-one percent of guys say they are confused about whether or not girls want them to initiate sex.[5]

- More than three-quarters of guys (78 percent) agree that there is "way too much pressure" from society to have sex.[6]

- Fifty-five percent of males and 54 percent of females aged fifteen to nineteen have engaged in oral sex with someone of the opposite sex.[7]

- Daily pornographic search engine requests: sixty-eight million (25 percent of total search engine requests).[8]

- Each year there are approximately nineteen million new STD infections, and almost half of them are among youth aged fifteen to twenty-four.[9]

- ☯ "In the 1960s one out of every sixty sexually active teens got an STD.... Today one in four sexually active teenagers is infected."[10]

- ☯ "Today, 8-18 year-olds devote an average of 7 hours and 38 minutes...to using entertainment media across a typical day (more than 53 hours a week). And because they spend so much of that time 'media multitasking' (using more than one medium at a time), they actually manage to pack a total of 10 hours and 45 minutes...worth of media content into those 7½ hours."[11]

Point well taken. We see it, but we may not realize the media tsunami is quite this extreme. I mean, I know *my* kids don't immerse themselves in media for more than ten hours a day! I am sure that is *not* my child. Although we may agree wholeheartedly on that, we as parents need to take some intentional steps to make certain these statistics don't come to represent our children as the pressure to conform to our culture tightens its grip. I am convinced this generation has a calling to live lives that are nothing short of revolutionary when compared to the current state of our culture.

The reason I am such an advocate of telling parents the facts is that I speak to thousands of Christian parents on a regular basis. I am startled by the sheer number of well-intentioned parents who thought they were protecting their children from these influences and yet who stand in tears as they share about discovering their son's addiction to pornography, their daughter's pregnancy at seventeen, or the fact that their preschooler was molested by a teen during Sunday school.

Heart-wrenching stories for sure. It's this culture making itself at home in our living rooms. It's the enemy having victory in the dark and secret places of hearts that are not under the lordship of Jesus Christ. Is there an answer to this problem? What do we do when these lies of the world slither under our front doors and into our child's bedroom?

God created the family to be a light in the darkness and to have victory over the enemy. He created the family before the church. God designed the family as a key center for the overflow of His Spirit into the lives of those around us. This is why Satan has targeted the family, especially our children, for destruction.

*We need to be on the offensive and gaining ground in our kids' hearts and minds that the enemy is trying to steal.*

But who wins in the end? God does. When we want to save our kids from the destruction the enemy intends for them, we have to realize that God Almighty, who reigns and lives forever and has the final victory, is the one backing us up. He is behind us in this effort. He brings victory to bear against all that is trying to defeat us. The power of His Spirit will overcome all the attacks of the enemy.

So does that mean we can sit back and do nothing? No. We are in a battle, and our children's very souls are at stake. We need to begin fighting on behalf of this generation. The weapons of this warfare are many, and they are straight from the hand of God. From the time our kids are young, we need to familiarize ourselves with how to engage in this battle. We need to be on the offensive and gaining ground in our kids' hearts and minds that the enemy is trying to steal. Far too many well-meaning parents wait until the enemy has moved in and stolen territory belonging to God before engaging in this battle.

Parents need to actively, intentionally weigh in on all these agendas that our culture brings to bear. It doesn't matter how our parents talked with us. Today the battle is very different, and we need to engage if our children are going to rise up and answer the call to turn the tide of this culture back to Christ. Study after study shows that there is a significant difference when we do.

> ♥ "...if adults merely provide adolescents with facts about behavior, but don't give them guidance on how to act on this

information, teens and young adults cannot make the very best decisions and often will make poor decisions."[12]

🔒 "Lower rates of adolescent sexual activity are associated with having parents who demonstrate a combination of traditional attitudes toward sexual behavior and effective communication practices, with positive relationships, a sense of acceptance by the adolescent, and with higher levels of family attachment, involvement, and supervision."[13]

🔒 "More than nine in 10 [teens] note that abstaining from sexual activity in high school results in having respect for yourself and enjoying the respect of your family."[14]

🔒 "Adolescents whose mothers discussed the social and moral consequences of being sexually active are less likely to engage in sexual intercourse."[15]

🔒 "Children whose parents monitor them more closely are less likely to be sexually active when they are in their teens. Adolescents whose parents report stricter monitoring of their children's behaviors during preadolescence are 30 percent less likely to be sexually active when compared to adolescents whose parents reported less strict monitoring of their children's behaviors during preadolescence."[16]

🔒 "Teens whose parents watch television with them more frequently and limit their TV viewing are less likely to be sexually active."[17]

🔒 "Adolescents whose parents talk with them about standards of sexual behavior are more likely to be abstinent. Youths whose parents talked to them about what is right and wrong in sexual behavior were significantly more likely to be abstinent than peers whose parents did not."[18]

Parents, whether your kids are four or fourteen, you are the number one influence in their lives. You have the potential to influence them both negatively and positively. After a nationwide study on teenagers (the National Study of Youth and Religion), researchers came to this conclusion: "Adults inescapably exercise immense influence in the lives of teens—positive and negative, passive and active. The question therefore is not whether adults exert influence, but what kinds of influence they exert."[19]

To raise a pure generation, we as parents must see how critical our role is in our children's lives. We need to take responsibility for imparting to them God's plan for their purity of hearts, minds, and bodies and not let our culture squeeze them into its mold by default. Just as we take other areas of our kids' upbringing—such as their academics and gifting—seriously, we need to chart a course for the development of their character in purity so they can stand against the tide of this culture.

We need to give them a vision that comes from the throne room of heaven. We need to impart to them that God, the Creator of this universe, has a more awesome love story than Hollywood could ever create. After all, He is the ultimate Creator. This task may seem hard, because it will require us to communicate with them in a way that our parents may never have spoken to us. But the good news is this: God is for us; He will provide the wisdom, endurance, and help that we need. We can lean upon the instruction He has given us to pass along His principles to our children.

Your children have been given an invitation to be a part of a world-changing, pure generation. And they are looking to you, mom and dad, to help them answer this amazing calling. Are you willing?

# Chapter 1

# THE EVER-CHANGING LANDSCAPE OF TECHNOLOGY

I F ANYTHING HAS changed since we were kids, it's the world of technology. (Remember when cell phones were the size of your tennis shoe?) The funny thing is, it doesn't matter what generation you represent; technology changes so fast it makes an impact on all of us—especially our kids. Yet our children seem to navigate all these changes so easily. It's as if they are natives in a digital world, while we parents are immigrants.[1] The landscape is familiar to them, and for us oftentimes it is foreign territory with new language, customs, and social mores.

Look at how quickly this world of technology

has changed over the past few decades. (Sure, top secret agents used these toys for years before they landed in the hands of us common folk, but for the majority of us, here are the dates we had access to them):

- Desktop computers were the wave of the future in the 1980s.

- We thought we had "arrived" with the floppy disk in 1984.

- Cell phones made our lives easier by the 1990s.

- The Internet changed our world in the late 1990s.

- The first commercial text message was sent in 1992.

- The iPod revolution came on the scene in 2001.

- In 2006 the word *google* was added to the *Merriam Webster Collegiate Dictionary*.

- By 2008 the number of text messages sent daily exceeded the current population of the planet.

- In 2009, 95 percent of downloaded songs were downloaded illegally.

- That same year the average American teen sent and received 2,272 text messages every month. By 2010 the average went up to 3,339.

- In 2010, 6.1 trillion text messages were sent and received. As of 2011, there were only 7 billion people alive.
- It is now estimated that a week's worth of the *New York Times* contains more information than a person was likely to come across in a lifetime in the eighteenth century.
- And by 2013 the long-awaited "supercomputer" is expected to surpass the computational capabilities of the human brain.

Now check out how quickly it took the following things to reach a market audience of fifty million:

- Radio: thirty-eight years
- TV: thirteen years
- Internet: four years
- iPod: three years
- Facebook: two years[2]

So what does it all mean? In one generation we have gone from the Stone Age to the Space Age technologically, and it is continuing to grow exponentially.

The book of Daniel talks about knowledge increasing (Dan. 12:4). The sheer volume of information that our kids deal with is massive. With information, advice, and guidance multiplying on the earth so rapidly, how do we know who is influencing our kids?

Many parents I have met use this feeling of being in a different world as an excuse to not engage on this level with their children. I hear people say all the time, "I don't understand any of that stuff, so I don't even go there!" I have to admit, I am no tech whiz either, but if we don't "go there," we will be forfeiting one of our greatest opportunities not only to parent our children but also to disciple them in this area of their lives. This is an arena where I see the enemy lurking, just waiting to snatch our kids over to the dark side before they have even left the "safety" of our living rooms.

When we were kids, we had to go to the mall or out to a restaurant to see our friends; now our own children just hop on their computers or mini-computers (i.e., cell phones) to do the same thing. Sure, there were ways for us to get into mischief, but usually that did not happen under the same roof, let alone the same room that our parents were sitting in! Now kids don't even have to walk out the door to get themselves into trouble.

- One in five teens have sent/posted a nude/ semi-nude picture or video of themselves.[3]

- One in three teen boys have had nude/ semi-nude images sent to them that were originally meant for someone else.[4]

- The average age of first Internet exposure to porn is age eleven.[5]

- One in three visitors to pornographic websites are women.[6]

We parents have to realize that being online is like being in a house with no parents home. We would never let our kids throw a party at our house with no holds barred, but when we let them online with no boundaries, it is the same thing. We have to understand that we need to be training our kids from the time they are young to protect their purity of heart, mind, and body when it comes to technology. We need to teach them that who they really are is who they are when no one is watching.

You know the saying, "What happens in Vegas, stays in Vegas"? Well that's how our kids view the Internet. They think that they can go on a "virtual moral vacation" anytime they want, without any consequences. They think no one will ever find out what they do online. And it's easy for us, as parents, to think that the online activity of our kids isn't that big a deal—after all, most of their friends are doing the same things. This apathy toward the online behavior of our kids could be for many reasons, but I believe a huge one is because the consequences of high-risk online behavior are often delayed. Think about it. You know what's going on if you come home after visiting family over the weekend and there is clear evidence throughout the whole house that your son threw a wild party. You have reason to suspect something when your daughter, normally bubbly and cheerful, suddenly becomes withdrawn and depressed, and then you find out from a friend's mom that she's been seen alone with the school's playboy. Yet often high-risk online behavior is more difficult to detect and therefore more serious. The longer negative patterns go on, the stronger and deeper they get. You owe it to your children to monitor their online activity. It could literally have lifelong consequences if they are allowed free rein on the Internet.

## STEALING THE TIME OF A GENERATION

The enemy has a plan for this generation, and it is to steal and destroy. I am convinced that the enemy will use technology to steal away a generation along with their destiny. When kids (and especially teens) spend hours playing video games, chatting online on social networking sites, texting on their cell phones, or watching every movie that has been released this past decade, their time has been wasted. That same time could have been spent on training for their future. We parents must realize that we use technology differently than our children do. We usually use technology as a means to an end, not an end in itself. While we are task-oriented online, our kids go online for the sole purpose of just hanging out there.

At Generations of Virtue we have a six-week World Changers Intensive internship program for seventeen- to twenty-one-year-olds. This is an unforgettable time for these young people to dive deep into purity, holiness, servanthood, and ministry. One thing we ask is that they "unplug" for the six weeks that they are with us. They are not allowed to have their cell phones or computers except to call home once a week. The young people return home after their six-week "media fast" new and different people. They realize that unplugging isn't such a bad idea after all and that it can really aid in getting their hearts and minds focused on their purpose, their calling, and their personal relationship with Jesus Christ. But even more striking to me is how many young people I speak to that will not apply for the internship because they cannot bring all their gadgets with them.

There are many other opportunities that I see young people missing because their tech world would not be intact. I see them forgoing opportunities to do missions work around the world, because in some areas they won't be able to check their social networks or text their best friends. I see young people who won't leave their video games long enough to help out with ministry opportunities right in their own cities. This is why I say the enemy is stealing the destiny of a generation. While they sit at their computers playing online role-playing games, the enemy is not only stealing their hearts and minds but also the hearts and minds of those they could be reaching as well.

Parents must realize what their children are forgoing when they pour themselves wholeheartedly into their very own "media empire." God has designed this time for young people to learn, grow, and be discipled in their calling. But oftentimes, by the time young adults reach their midtwenties, media and culture have done most of the shaping, instead of godly influences. I like to tell young people the old saying that "time is money." In your bank account of life what are you investing in? Are you investing in your future, your calling, your destiny, or are you investing in things that will not profit your future whatsoever?

## REAL LIFE: REAL RELATIONSHIPS

Another area in which parents need to mentor their children in is the area of healthy relationships. Kids are extremely comfortable in a virtual world. They have virtual friends from around the globe. While parents use social networks as an opportunity to network with old friends they have personally known from high school, college, and present, their kids strive to add a multitude of "friends" whether or not they have ever met them. This might lead to a son or daughter accepting their friend's neighbor's cousin's brother as a friend—someone whom they have never met in real life!

The dilemma with this is that while teens are on a quest to accept more and more friends for the sake of popularity, their relational world shifts the balance from real to virtual. They exchange real, authentic, face-to-face relationships for virtual illusion, false impressions, and even delusion.

The point I am making here is twofold. First, the more virtual relationships our kids have with people they have not met face-to-face, the more jeopardy they are in. It is a rule at our home that they have to have spent time with someone face-to-face before they add them to their friends list on any networking site they are on. This way we at least know the friends really are who they say they are.

When we meet people for the first time, we often try to discern what type of person they are. Even with people we have known for years but don't know well, we are usually observing what they say and how they act to see if this is someone we'd like to have in our lives. We do this by using at least two of the five senses that we have—seeing and hearing. But with virtual relationships, we don't have either of these options available to us. Sure we may "see," but we are seeing only an image, the image the other person wants to project to the world. Many times that image is different from the real person. It's nothing more than a mask. We want our kids to have relationships with people in which they can learn to discern who that person really is without the mask.

Secondly and most importantly is that real relationships happen in real life. The healthiest relationships are built face-to-face, day in and day out, not virtually. Real life is real relationships. Now I know there are some reading this who have even met their spouses virtually before being introduced in person. I know that virtual relationships are a part of our world. It's just that our kids need to establish and anchor themselves in relationships that are not only virtual. Because of the push for popularity, both for the shy and the outgoing, virtual relationships have such an appeal to teens that some teens would rather live primarily in that world than in the reality of everyday life. The shy ones like it because they can be different from the way they are in school every day, and the extroverts like it because they live for the thrill of relationship—the more the merrier.

As parents we need to be focused on the fact that no matter where technology takes us, we still want to be anchored in the face-to-face relationships, where learning how to deal with the good, the bad, and the ugly in other people takes place in a consistent, loving, everyday, face-to-face environment. We need to teach our kids that when they get frustrated with their future spouses, they can't just hit the "delete" button to end the relationship. Real relationships take hard work, day in and day out. The truth is that our spouses have to live with not just the good impressions we make, but rather with the real us.

## THE WORSHIP FACTOR

This is another factor we want to be aware of with our kids and their virtual worlds. Many young people have mixed motives for being online all the time. Now it's not that they are aware on the surface that this is a motivation, but it is our job as parents to disciple them in a way that purifies their motives for being online. The bottom line is that they like the attention they get from others. Whether it is that online game they are winning or the social networking site and their thousands of friends, they like the fact that this is a "world" where people like them. Teens live in a world of growing maturity and constant challenges. Teens have a fair amount of conflict with parents and other authorities as they are challenged to mature and forge a place for their individual identity. It's a stretching experience that can be downright uncomfortable. Then along comes an opportunity not only to have people like the things they do but also to be the center of attention as well. I call this the "worship factor," or the "me factor." Does this sound familiar to you?—"It's all about me and my friends and what I do."

I have a young lady on my staff with Generations of Virtue who prayed for over three years about having a Facebook account. Every time she would ask the Lord about getting on and having her own account, she would feel a check in her spirit. God began to show her that her motives were not right. She said that God convicted her that it was difficult enough for her to put Him first and that this would be a place where she would be pointing people to her, rather than the Lord. She said she had enough trouble trying to keep God as the focus and not her, as it was, and this would only make it harder. Finally there came a point where God dealt with the motivation of her heart so she would be able to use this area of technology to advance His kingdom purposes and not her own little empire of self.

This is the online worship factor. Is it all

about me or about truly being a representative of God's mighty army and making advances for His kingdom? So much of technology centers around my life, my pictures, my friends, my little world. What happened to our calling and destiny to be world-changers for the almighty King? We get sucked into this vortex of self and the "me" factor that is all about me getting worship from my friends. Last I read in the Bible, Lucifer fell from heaven because he wanted the worship that belonged to God.

## ADVANCING GOD'S KINGDOM

In his book *Re-Create: Building a Culture in Your Home Stronger Than the Culture Deceiving Your Kids*, Ron Luce says that "98 percent of our population are followers of culture and 2 percent are the shapers of culture."[7] In a world where our kids are incredibly tech-savvy, why don't we encourage them to become the 2 percent? That 2 percent has tremendous power and authority over our culture. If that 2 percent were young people sold out to God's purposes of advancing His kingdom, that would truly rock our world. Look what twelve disciples did without the Internet! If we work with this next generation, the ones living in our own homes, and give them a vision for the impact they can have on this world through technology, there's no envisioning how God will use it. If they write the music, direct the movies, create the websites, engineer the games, and manage their Internet world with pure hands and a clean heart to advance God's kingdom, this world will never be the same. This is the vision that we have to communicate to them: if their motives are pure and they see technology as a way to advance God's kingdom, and not their mini-empires, this will create change.

Not that technology and media are bad—just the opposite! However, this powerful tool has been hijacked by the enemy of our souls, and we must take back the ground that the enemy has stolen and use it for the glory of God.

## EVERYDAY PRACTICAL HINTS

Now whether your kids are three or thirteen, there are some practical measures you can take to make their technology world much safer. You have to start when your kids are young so you can be up to speed by the time they reach their teen years when technology issues really come to the forefront.

The number one suggestion I give to all parents, no matter what age their kids are, is to put some kind of filtering or monitoring software on all computers that kids have access to. This will save you from a path of destruction that the enemy is betting your kids will stumble into. One of the most common experiences that hundreds of parents have shared with me is how their son or daughter chanced upon some kind of pornographic website by accident, then became addicted. This dark world is proactively seeking to imprison your child for life. Filtering software provides an outer perimeter that at least helps guard them from this onslaught.

Now I am no computer whiz. My kids are the ones to save me most of the time from my technology mishaps and woes—anything from my e-mail not working to my printer being jammed. As I stated earlier, they are the natives in this territory. Still, I make it a point to find a way to put filtering software on our computer and learn how to monitor it properly. Mind you, it is not enough to have it, if you do not know how to monitor it and use it properly. You need to come to grips with how to use the software once it is in place, and if this is way beyond your realm of expertise, don't use that as an excuse to hand your kids over to the enemy on a silver platter. Find a technologically capable college student from your church, and have them install the filtering program and teach you how to use it.

There are no excuses when it comes to this world of pornography. Take a look at what we are up against:

🔒 Pornographic websites: 4.2 million (12 percent of total websites)

- Pornographic pages: 420 million

- Daily pornographic search engine requests: 68 million (25 percent of total search engine requests)

- Daily pornographic e-mails: 2.5 billion (8 percent of total e-mails)

- Average daily pornographic e-mails/user: 4.5 per Internet users

- Monthly pornographic downloads (peer-to-peer): 1.5 billion (35 percent of all downloads)

- Websites offering illegal child pornography: 100,000

- Sexual solicitations of youth made in chat rooms: 89 percent

- Youths who received sexual solicitation: one in seven

- Worldwide visitors to pornographic websites: 72 million monthly[8]

No matter what age your children are, it is a good idea to keep computers in public, high-traffic areas of your home. Remember laptops have legs and like to walk away. Keeping computer screens where they can be seen by other eyes will cut down on temptation. Especially at night, keep all these devices inaccessible by blocking the Internet signal or placing them in your bedroom. (I know one dad who actually unplugs the router and takes it into his bedroom every night.) One of the most common stories parents share with me is about kids getting online, via computers or cell phones or other devices, in the middle of the night while the world is sleeping.

Time limits are also important. Whether it is for playing games or being on Facebook, studies show that parents who set time limits see results:

> Only about three in ten young people say they have rules about how much time they can spend watching TV (28%) or playing video games (30%), and 36% say the same about using the computer. But when parents *do* set limits, children spend less time with media: those with *any* media rules consume nearly 3 hours less media per day (2:52) than those with no rules.[9]

Don't forget that cell phones are essentially small computers, and every generation of phone gets more and more powerful. Oftentimes we focus on the actual laptop or desktop, but many times this is not what gets our kids in trouble. They are just as comfortable using their cell phones to have access to all the garbage on the Internet as well. A recent study on media use among teens revealed "young people now spend more time listening to music, playing games, and watching TV on their cell phones (a total of :49 [minutes] daily) than they spend *talking* on them (:33 [minutes])"[10] Being familiar with your carrier's parental control options and always picking the phone that is the simplest and most basic for your child's needs is imperative. Although we parents might not use every feature on our phones, our kids will figure out what those features are and learn how to use them. Don't assume that because you don't, they won't. Remember they are the natives when it comes to this technology!

Now it is no easy task to find our kids (especially kids under the age of fifteen) phones that do not have every cutting-edge feature, bell, and whistle. I went the other day to find my fourteen-year-old daughter a phone that would simply make calls, send text messages, and take decent pictures, and there were only a handful of crummy models to choose from at our carrier's store. Most of them looked like something we would plan on getting Grandma, with large print screens. It made me want to just cave in and get her the newest model of the iPhone; I mean, she is a very responsible young lady! But the words of so many teens and parents echoed in my head about scenarios that came up with their "good, responsible" kids being drawn into temptation that they were not ready to handle. And the problem is that once that happens, you can't go back. So our search goes on for a simple phone, one that is still cool!

Nothing is more crushing than finding out that your child is immersed in pornography. This is a common occurrence that parents

*Don't expect your kids to be able to stand and win if you are not engaged yourself in a conquest for victory.*

tearfully experience. Pornography is an attack of the enemy especially focused on derailing our sons, but daughters fall prey to it as well. It is evil, and there is a proactive offensive being launched against our children.

- "Roughly two-thirds (67 percent) of young men and one-half (49 percent) of young women agree that viewing pornography is acceptable."[11]

- Boys between the ages of twelve and seventeen who regularly view pornography on the Internet had sex at an earlier stage in their lives and were more likely to initiate oral sex, apparently imitating what they had watched.[12]

- "More than half of sexually experienced guys would rather give up sex for a month than give up going online for a month."[13]

- "Overall revenue from the porn industry in the United States is greater than the

National Football League, National Basketball Association, and Major League Baseball combined."[14]

🔒 Seventy percent of sexual advances over the Internet happened while youngsters were on a home computer.[15]

🔒 Ninety percent of eight- to sixteen-year-olds have viewed porn online (most while doing homework).[16]

Our kids need to be equipped to win this battle. We cannot stand by and assume that they will not be affected by this enemy. They need to be dressed for battle and be well acquainted with the enemy and his tactics. Now a word to parents: don't expect your kids to be able to stand and win if you are not engaged yourself in a conquest for victory. If pornography is an issue in your life, this is the time to leave it at the cross and get squared around. If for nothing else, do it for the children you love so dearly. The enemy of your soul will convince you this is impossible, but God is the only hope in the war being waged against your soul. Surrender this area to the Lord minute by minute so the generational line of your family can be redirected into the godly line of sons that are meant to stand in this war.

In his book *Hero: Becoming the Man She Desires*, Fred Stoeker (coauthor of the Every Man's Battle series) asks, "Are you leaving the women in your life better off for having known you?"[17] Is that true of you, Dad? Is that true of your sons?

Although pornography is primarily a male issue, women are becoming more and more involved. Fred Stoeker is a good friend of mine. As a guest speaker at a parent-teen conference called ReConnect that my ministry hosts, Fred shared a story that shocked me. He had been invited to speak at a popular Bible college, and a week before his arrival the school had sent an anonymous poll to the students regarding their pornography usage. His question wasn't, "When was the last time you viewed pornography?" It was, "How often do you view pornography?" The poll results were unsettling to say the least; 100 percent of men and 87 percent of women said they view pornography at least once a week.

We need to prepare our children age-appropriately for this dilemma. We need to equip them for this battle. Most boys are shown their first pornography at age eleven, but this is becoming more common even as young as age eight.[18] How do we brace ourselves for this, let alone our children? Start by explaining to your young children that if they ever see a picture anywhere (on the computer, in a book, magazine, even a movie) of a woman (or a man) who is not properly dressed, especially one without clothes on, to come and tell you immediately. Part of the key I have found in waging this battle is to bring things out into the light. Things kept hidden in darkness provide the enemy with a door of entrance. In teaching our kids to be upfront and tell the truth, we are allowing the light of God to shine into that area and bring redemption. Leaving things in secret gives the enemy the edge and the upper hand.

Also explain to your child how to handle this issue online. For this generation, pornography is relentless at trying to trap our kids when they are innocently browsing the Internet. Explain to them that if they ever see anything online that depicts a person without clothes on or doing something that makes them uncomfortable or is inappropriate, they should immediately close the page and run to get you. Further, I always recommend that they turn off the computer, because I don't want the unsuspecting brother or sister to walk by and be scarred as the first child is running to find a parent! You can always go back later and research how that image came up on the screen. Now I always advise parents to take a deep breath, put on an un-alarming demeanor, and go see what's up. Reacting by screaming at the top of your lungs and popping your eyeballs out will hardly encourage your child that you are approachable when these kinds of issues come up.

Parents, we need to be engaged in this even when our children don't come and tell us that they have found suspicious content online. One time when we were doing a teen program with about four hundred teens in Arizona, a fourteen-year-old boy came up and quietly shared his testimony with me. He said that he had stumbled onto pornography online, and out of curiosity he had looked at it a bit one day, although he knew better. He went to bed without sharing with his parents what kind of content he had viewed on the Internet. After falling sound asleep, he was awakened by both his parents and confronted with his activity. After much discussion late into the night, and a time of prayer and repentance, he went back to sleep with a clear conscience. He confessed that having his parents do that changed the course of his life. He was proud to share that he had not looked at pornography again. His parents, by loving him enough to be aware of his online activities and confronting him with the truth, had saved him from a world of conflict and hidden sin. But to catch this hidden conduct right away, it took parents who not only had filtering software but also monitored it as well.

As much as we need to train our children to be on guard when they are young, we need also to set their sights on purity of mind, heart, and body as they get older. They need to be able to stand against their flesh, which is set on pushing the boundaries. Our teens are immersed in a world where sleaze and promiscuity are common, and to say no to this onslaught will surely put them in the minority. It is essential to help them see that this is really a step into God's higher calling.

I have listed several resources at the end of this chapter that we at Generations of Virtue have found useful. Work through them with your teens so that they can overcome the battle set before them. This battle with media exposure is an everyday battle. The enemy has declared war against our children, and we need not only to acknowledge the battle but also engage in the everyday scrimmages to ensure victory.

**Resource for dads:**

🔒 *Every Man's Battle* by Stephen Arterburn and Fred Stoeker with Mike Yorkey

**Resources for dads and sons:**

🔒 *Hero: Becoming the Man She Desires* by Fred Stoeker and Jasen Stoeker

🔒 *Preparing Your Son for Every Man's Battle* by Stephen Arterburn and Fred Stoeker, with Mike Yorkey

🔒 *Tactics: Securing the Victory in Every Young Man's Battle* by Fred Stoeker with Mike Yorkey

**Resources for moms and daughters:**

- *Every Young Woman's Battle* by Shannon Ethridge and Stephen Arterburn

- *What Are You Waiting For?* by Dannah Gresh

# Chapter 2

# HOLLYWOOD HANGOVER

S TUDIES SHOW THAT the average child spends more than fifty-three hours a week with media.[1] That is about the same amount of time that most adults spend at their full-time jobs. With the cascading river of media flowing into our living rooms, how can we control the flood? This flood of media is seeping all over the house and into every area of our lives.

- ✚ About two-thirds (64 percent) of young people say the TV is usually on during meals.

- ✚ Just under half (45 percent) say the TV is left on "most of the time" in their home, even if no one is watching.

- Seven in ten (71 percent) have a TV in their bedroom.

- Half (50 percent) have a console video game player in their room.[2]

When I first read this, I thought this applied only to teenagers, but this study addresses eight-year-olds through eighteen-year-olds. Tweens are becoming some of the greatest consumers of media. Media use increases substantially when children hit the eleven- to fourteen-year-old age group, an increase that breaks down this way:

- One hour, twenty-two minutes more TV viewing

- One hour, fourteen minutes more music

- One hour more computer time

- Twenty-four minutes more playing video games

- Total media exposure of eleven hours, fifty-three minutes per day (vs. seven hours fifty-one minutes for eight- to ten-year-olds).[3]

Thinking I could breathe a sigh of relief, I assumed that young children were not affected by this trend. I was wrong. Look at the numbers for our littlest ones:

♦ A third of all children six years old and younger (36 percent) have a TV in their bedrooms.

♦ One in four (27 percent) has their own VCR or DVD player.

♦ One in ten has a video game player, and 7 percent have a computer.

♦ Thirty percent of children three years old and younger have a TV in their rooms.

♦ Forty-three percent of four- to six-year-olds have a TV in their rooms.

♦ Children six years old and younger spend almost two hours a day with screen media (including TV, movies, video games, and the computer)[4]

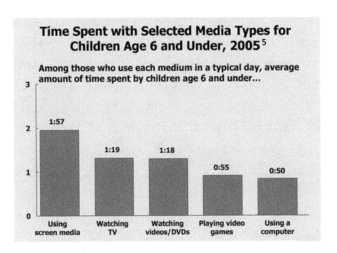

**Time Spent with Selected Media Types for Children Age 6 and Under, 2005**[5]

Among those who use each medium in a typical day, average amount of time spent by children age 6 and under...

| Using screen media | Watching TV | Watching videos/DVDs | Playing video games | Using a computer |
|---|---|---|---|---|
| 1:57 | 1:19 | 1:18 | 0:55 | 0:50 |

Obviously these types of media are everywhere, so how do we protect our kids? What kind of dam can we build to hold back the deluge of media? We need to construct some kind of protection around our families so we can be the ones to open or close the flow that cascades into our homes.

With the flood of media increasing at such an astounding rate, the enemy intends to sweep our children away with the sheer volume of messages that inculcate the lies of this world. Satan knows that the intensity of the lies of the media works in his favor to further his cause. The mind that is not established in Christ and fortified by the Holy Spirit is subject to this tsunami. A child's mind that receives all this negative content will establish all these lies as a foundation in truth instead of the truth of the Lord Jesus Christ. As parents, we have to intentionally fight this battle on a daily basis. The way our children's brains are being wired and growing each day creates a structure to either hold the truth of God or the lies of this world. What are we doing in the midst of this onslaught of media messages to create a foundation of truth?

As much as I sometimes want to chuck the cell phone, trash the computer and TV, and move to a secluded cabin in the Rockies with no Internet or cable service, this is not feasible in our world. We have to deal with the barrage of media. We have to teach our children to have healthy boundaries and attitudes toward all the information and the electronics that were never available to us when we grew up.

A good place to start with each one of our families is an assessment. We need to come to grips with the amount of media flow that is coming into our homes. Use the example table at the end of this chapter to monitor the media each family member digests in any given week. Reassess periodically to see how the various forms of media are coming into your home and robbing you of your time and values. Every time I sit down to do this exercise, I am surprised by how much more media usage slithers into our home than I am aware of. It quietly extends its presence in each of our homes (because, besides when they're sleeping, our kids are quietest when they are consuming media!). It wants to reside with us and stay. Even we parents—how often do we grab our phone or computer to catch up on e-mail or Facebook first thing in the morning before reaching for our Bible?

We need to be an example to the next generation. Can we unplug periodically? Do we even demonstrate to our kids this is possible?

*It doesn't work to just block the messages of this world unless we are pouring in the real truth and power of the Lord Jesus Christ.*

We need to assess the ways that God's truth is taking hold of our lives. Where are we making space for this foundation of truth to be built? How much are we allowing the world to set the standards, and what are we doing to tilt the balance of media to undergird our family with the mind of Christ and the power of God? It doesn't work to just block the messages of this world unless we are pouring in the real truth and power of the Lord Jesus Christ. This is an amazing opportunity for us as parents to "teach God's truths diligently to your children, talking of them when we sit in our houses, when we walk by the way, when we lie down, and when we rise up" (Deut. 6:7, paraphrased).

## GUARDING OUR HOMES

You are the gatekeeper of your home. You are the one who rations the amount of media crashing through the floodgates. At the same time, within our homes we need to saturate our kids with the Word of God. While our kids are young, this can be accomplished in several ways.

While our kids are babies, toddlers, and in preschool, we need to be creative as we saturate their hearts with the Word of God and His foundation of truth. Children's minds are like sponges at this age and will soak up whatever is in their environment. Take this opportunity to have your kids do a lot of listening to the Word of God. Although

Bible stories for kids are great, I also have my kids listen to the Word of God straight from the Bible. I play the Bible softly in their rooms while they go to sleep. At family devotions we make a point of listening to the Bible as well.

Bible audios are one thing that I can let my kids listen to and not have to worry about questionable content. But what do we do about everything else? Well, media discernment is a skill that can be taught and developed from a young age. The little things we do at the preschool stage really matter. For example, when my girls watch a movie such as *Cinderella*, I talk to them about what's going on in the movie. In every Disney movie the main characters always kiss. I might be trying to get dinner on the table and they are watching *Cinderella* for the millionth time, but when it comes to the kissing part, I always say, "That prince and princess, they are kissing. Are they married? Should they be kissing?" My girls will respond with "No! They're not married yet!" I always want them to assess the messages (or lies) that are presented as truth so they are not just taking it in, hook, line, and sinker. They need to understand that the stories they see on TV and movies that seem so "happily ever after" are rarely true to reality.

When children are young, we need to be watchful of what is broadcasting from the TV in the background of our homes. With close to half of all households having the TV on all the time, we need to realize what impact this has on our children. We even need to be careful with the news. I know many of our homes have cable news streaming into them 24/7. News stories can traumatize young children because of the way their brains develop. When we adults watch news programming, our brains can understand that a segment of the plane crashing into the World Trade Center on 9/11 is just a replay, but a two- to seven-year-old may think it is happening again and again.[6] They don't comprehend time and space sequentially yet. Even children up to ten or eleven may not understand spatial differences enough to know that the war images on the news are in the Middle East and not down the street. This becomes overwhelming to them when events from around the world are projected around them at such an overstimulating rate.

My husband, Kay, is involved in humanitarian work around the world and needs to know the news as it is happening. He typically first hears of disasters around the world via the news and then gets his disaster teams going. Since he works primarily out of our home, he makes sure to stream the news only in his office. He remains alert to the possibility of one of our younger children walking in, so he can turn it off if it has any content of concern. He also does not leave the TV on when he steps away from his office.

As our kids move into the elementary years, it is up to us as parents to decide how wide we want to allow the media gate to stay open. With our children interacting with more and more kids, the floodgates will try to push open wider and wider. Use this season as an opportunity to teach media discernment in a greater way. Have discussions about advertising—not only about what companies are trying to sell you but also how they are doing it.

One day my eight-year-old daughter and I were watching TV, and a commercial came on about makeup. I asked her, "What are they trying to sell here?" and she replied that it was some kind of makeup. As the beautiful women pranced across the screen one by one, I asked her if I would look like one of them if I purchased the same product. With a look of shock on her face she said, "No, Mom, I don't think you would look like that!" It is so helpful for them to realize that not every product will get the same results as we see on TV. With today's ease of airbrushing and digital manipulation of images, sometimes I wonder if there are ever any "real live" people on our screens or in the print media we read!

Let's take another example: When you are driving down the freeway and see a billboard of that amazing sports car your son loves, use it as an opportunity to teach him about advertising. You might say something like, "Wow, that's a really amazing sports car!"

To which he would reply, "Yes, Mom, that's really cool!"

Next you might point out something like, "Does the beautiful woman standing next to that car come with the car when you buy it?" Or, "Do you get a date with her when you buy the car?" It is imperative that boys learn the role women have (how women are used as sexual objects) in advertising. Young men need to learn how to honor women and not treat them as objects in this sexualized culture that we live in.

Consider how it goes to watch sports on TV. I know that for a lot of dads, watching sports with their sons is a favorite pastime. It's not the actual sport that worries me; it's the commercials. At our house we have opted to just turn the TV off during the commercials or to record the sporting event so we don't have to watch them. I can't stress this enough when it comes to Super Bowl parties, especially when you include the half-time performances! (I'm thinking of "wardrobe malfunctions" and other debacles during this prime-time event.) This is a great time to go out and play some football. Even if you're having a blizzard at the moment, that is probably better than what they will see on TV!

Another quick tip regarding channel surfing. My husband and I joke that he likes to see what is on all four hundred cable channels during the ninety-second commercial break, while I would rather just endure the commercials not to miss any of the program I am currently watching. He is what you would call a "big picture" guy and wants to peruse everything else that is on. When our kids were young, we began to realize that what flashed across the screen during that split-second channel surfing could be very provocative, scary, or absurdly inappropriate! We made a commitment to each other not to channel surf when the kids were watching with us or popping in and out of the room.

## DEVELOPING MEDIA DISCERNMENT

As kids move into the teenage years, especially when they are between eleven and fifteen, their brains are at such a critical stage of development that the patterns they form will be a foundation for the rest of their lives. A 2008 study proved that what kids watch in TV and movies impacts their future actions. The more sexual content teens watched on television, the more likely they were to engage in sex over the next year, experimenting with the behaviors they had witnessed on TV.[7]

Alarmingly, the sexual content shown on television has gone up drastically since this study was concluded. If we were noticing the effects of sexual content on our children exposed to the media in 2008, how much higher is it today?

This is why, even when our kids' friends are viewing mature content such as PG-13 movies, we want to think twice before letting them watch too. We know the conclusion of the study: if kids are watching sexual content, they are going to pursue sexual activities. That puts us parents in a bind. It's not as if our teenagers are going to be content watching "innocent" G-rated movies throughout their teen years.

I have found a DVD player called ClearPlay to be extremely helpful here. ClearPlay filters out content such as sexuality, crude language, and violence, giving parents the ability to set limits and skip the scenes that are completely inappropriate. (Word of advice: make sure your kids don't forget to tell their friends that they saw certain movies on ClearPlay, or their friends' parents will be wondering if you have lost your mind letting them see *that* movie!) Go to my website, www .generationsofvirtue.org/techtips, to find out how ClearPlay can help your family.

Teaching your kids discernment when it comes to what they are watching is a key first step, starting when they are very young. Watch with them and help them see what reflects the truths of the Word of God versus the lies of our culture. Continue doing this throughout your kids' time at home with you.

"Butter and honey shall he eat, that he may know to refuse the evil, and choose the good" (Isa. 7:15, KJV). Just as we teach our kids about nutrition, we need to teach them how to give nutrients to their souls and spirits so they will know how to refuse the evil of our culture and choose the good things of God instead. Ask the Lord today what junk food in your media diet needs to be axed and what kind of nutrition you should add.

The following chart is a seven-day media evaluation, adapted from *Culture Shock: A Survival Guide for Teens.*[8] You can use it for every member of your family (Mom and Dad, you might have to help the little ones on this project). Once everyone has filled it out, come back together and assess your media intake.

| Activity / Day | Online Social Networking | Surfing the Web | On the Cell Phone / Texting | Listening to Music / Reading Magazines | Gaming / Video Games | Watching TV / Movies | Praying / Reading Bible |
|---|---|---|---|---|---|---|---|
| Day 1 | | | | | | | |
| Day 2 | | | | | | | |
| Day 3 | | | | | | | |
| Day 4 | | | | | | | |
| Day 5 | | | | | | | |
| Day 6 | | | | | | | |
| Day 7 | | | | | | | |

# Chapter 3

# THE ROOTS OF FAMILY CONNECTEDNESS

S EVERAL YEARS AGO we were on a family vacation in Marco Island, Florida. On the beach in front of our hotel a professional sand sculptor was working. Over the course of four days he sculpted a replica of the tower of London. This was no miniature model, either. It was about the size of our family's SUV, and the detail in the sculpture was incredible! Each day as his artwork was coming to life, my husband would strike up a conversation with him about his progress. The television channel Showtime was also on the scene taking moment-by-moment, time-lapse photos so they could highlight his efforts on their show.

At last the "sand castle" was complete. Cordoned off from the public, it was quite the masterpiece! The artist asked if our kids would be willing to help in the final efforts to put together the show. Confused, we asked what they could possibly assist with. He said that Showtime wanted them, on his command, to demolish the sculpture! We looked at him in disbelief. How could he allow a group of children to demolish what he had just spent days creating? When I looked closer at his face, I saw that he shared our concern. He went on to explain that it was Showtime that had come up with this plan, and to be the highlight of their documentary, he was willing to comply. He had never before torn down any sculpture he had designed.

Group of kids assembled, the cameras were ready to roll. The countdown ensued, and they were off. Running, scrambling, climbing, they tore down the majestic castle. The process of dismantling what had taken days to create took only minutes! What had been an extraordinary creation of unique design was demolished in a fraction of the time it had taken to construct it.

As God brought this experience back to my remembrance, I was reminded that it is much like the way we spend years building and sculpting our children. The formation of their character and destiny takes years to establish. Yet, just like that castle, all of this can be torn down in a matter of moments with one choice or a series of bad decisions.

It depends on what foundation we build on. Jesus exhorted us to build on the rock and not be like the foolish man who builds upon the sand (Matt. 7:24–27). Our culture has many "sandy" ideals. The only foundation that will stand is the rock of Jesus Christ and the Word of God. We need to raise the next generation to stand against the tide of culture, lest they be washed away with the waves of deceptive propaganda. We want to equip them to stand with the banner of Jesus Christ and God's eternal Word.

Parents, you are God's assigned instruments for raising up the next generation. Sure, there are other key mentors along the way, but I am convinced that when we get to heaven, God is not going to ask me how my child's teacher or nanny did. My husband and I are the ones responsible for raising our children. The buck stops with us. This is where God will equip us as parents, as we lean into His timeless wisdom to raise our children. And let me tell you, nothing has brought me to my knees more than raising my kids!

## FAMILY CONNECTEDNESS

Parents who are well connected with their kids provide the best protection from high-risk behavior. Studies show again and again that as our kids grow up, this is the most effective way to protect them against substance abuse, teen sexual activity, and negative choices.[1]

There are four additional keys that we can implement with our kids, no matter how young or old, that will have an immense impact on their future choices.

The first and most important key is *family connectedness* in the midst of today's world of endless opportunity and activity. Amid the chauffeuring, homework, church commitments, and work, family time has to win out. Sitting around the table together at dinner, family devotions, family vacations—it doesn't matter what form it takes, just think *family*!

In the midst of our hectic schedules this is quite a challenge, and I believe that is part of the enemy's plan. We encounter so many good opportunities, we miss God's best. In the end we have kids who can play a musical instrument with exquisite skill, take home the trophy for being the best in their sport, make great grades and graduate as valedictorian—but they don't have a dynamic relationship with Jesus Christ and the foundation of family. Don't get me wrong. It's not as if we have to give up these other opportunities; just prioritize what is God's best with a listening ear to Him. One day we will look at our kids and they will be grown up and off to college.

It happens all too fast, and we don't want to miss this window of opportunity!

Creating family connectedness takes planning and determination. Everything in our culture screams "peers" and individualism. Very little speaks of coming together as a family. One of the best decisions we have made as a family is to go on family ministry trips together. Whether it is for a weekend or two months, these trips have bonded us together in deep ways. Three times we have gone to Asia for several weeks to minister as a family. In the midst of new cultures, foreign languages, exotic food (try this with picky eaters!), and witnessing the beauty of the family of God around the world, our family connectedness has been forged in a very deep way.

Daily diligence in family connectedness is vital. Not all of us have the flexibility in our lives to embark on such a journey as I just mentioned. The bottom line is that it is the everyday connectedness that counts most. In our harried world it is important to connect with one another and God every day. We try to do this in our family devotion time. Now, not every day do we have time to do this, but at the least we try to pull together as a family and pray together. This takes just a few moments, but it brings enormous fruit. Sharing prayer requests and each praying to lift them up to our heavenly Father shifts burdens from our shoulders to His.

When our kids witness God answering prayer, it builds their faith. God created the family first, then the church. Therefore church begins at home.

## CLEAR EXPECTATIONS

Along with family connectedness there are three other keys discussed in these studies. Key number two is *clear expectations*. We parents must express clear expectations to our children. This includes being able to communicate when we disapprove of their actions or the actions of others. If we outline clear expectations ahead of time, our kids will think twice before they launch out into an unacceptable activity. When our kids want to go to a party, for example, we outline in advance what our expectations are. We ask whether parents will be present and if there is going to be any alcohol there. We ask very specifically what interactions will be going on between the sexes. We make our expectations for their behavior clear.

Studies show that especially when moms make their expectations clear about issues such as premarital sex, their children are likely to delay or not get entangled in them.[2] I imagine the only reason why dads are not included in this statistic is because they could not find enough available dads to survey. In general it is imperative to set very clear boundaries for our children when our kids are young and following throughout their teen years. If they do not hear the word *no*, they will not know how to use it themselves to create boundaries in their own situations.

## POSITIVE INPUT

The next key shown in these studies is *positive input*. Josh McDowell says:

Rules without relationship = rebellion
*while*
Relationship without rules = confusion.[3]

Balancing rules, any good parent-child relationship must provide positive feedback from parents to children. In order to grow and flourish, kids need the blessing of their parents just as much as they need clear parameters and expectations. We need to create for our children a path that they can navigate because it is clear and balanced. We need to work with them to build the "Highway of Holiness" that Isaiah 35:8 talks about. Along the way encouragement smooths the road as we get rid of the stones and character flaws and cast a vision for holiness.

## IMPORTANCE OF DADS

The last key is a father's involvement. I read a statistic once that girls are 250 percent more likely to become sexually active if their dad is not involved

in their lives on a predictable basis.[4] When I
shared that with my husband, his eyes grew wide
and he began to mutter, "Two hundred fifty percent! Two hundred fifty percent!"

You see, we have not one daughter, but five.
This absolutely rocked his world; he realized the
vital importance of his role. Now dads have a vital
role whether they have sons or daughters. They are
part of God's formula for molding and shaping
children. If you are a dad with many responsibilities, little extra time, and more than one child,
you may be overwhelmed when you read that
statement. My husband and I have found, in the
midst of our hectic schedules, that the key word
in this statement is "predictable." This is the goal
we aim for.

Dads can make predictable time even if they are
juggling many demands and responsibilities. My
husband travels for his work internationally and
within the United States, and yet he has done a
wonderful job spending predictable time with our
kids. He has found a way to do it that works for
him, and he accomplishes it in conjunction with
his everyday responsibilities.

Let me give you an example. He likes us to
have a clean car. Personally, because I am so busy
with all of the cooking, chauffeuring, laundry, and
schoolwork, making sure that our vehicles are
spotless and gleaming does not fall at the top of

my priority list. However, this is important to him. So in the dividing up of our household duties, the washing of the cars fell in his lap. He took this as an opportunity to spend time with one of his daughters. Ever since our now fourteen-year-old was two, he would plop her in the car, and they would be on their way to the car wash.

Now in Colorado where we live, most of the car washes are a small stand-alone gizmo behind the gas station. They would fuel up, and he would go in and visit the mini mart to buy her a healthy snack. (Something such as doughnuts and chocolate milk! Not exactly Mom's pick, but my daughter loved it.) Then they would drive into the car wash, and while the deluxe wash cycle was progressing, they would have their little heart-to-heart talks. It doesn't appear to be much, but add up two cars being washed on average two times a month over the years, and it equals predictable. My daughter knew that even if Dad was traveling, when he came home there would be a car that needed his attention and a daughter who did as well.

Whether it means going to the hardware store or getting the car washed, spending predictable time with our kids in the routine tasks that have to be accomplished is an objective that can be met by most dads. We don't have to wait to take our kids to Disneyland; we just need to incorporate them in our everyday activities on a predictable basis.

*A note to single moms: God knows the situation that you face, and He is going to provide everything necessary for you to raise both your sons and daughters. When dad is not available, God never leaves us destitute. He is our provider, and He is the provider for our children as well. Since there is never enough time for the work that has to be accomplished, take some of the tips from the previous section and incorporate them with your children as well.*

My husband is outstanding at having a special everyday activity that he does with each of our children. I told you about the one he takes to the car wash. He takes another one when he gets his haircut, and one he takes to get the special bird food. You get the picture. He incorporates spending time with his children into the chores and tasks he has to do anyway. This way they do not get missed when duty calls. This approach creates extra space for our children when life demands too much of our time just to keep it running.

For all of us our day runs out too quickly, and each of these four keys takes time. We have to see that the time we sow now each day with our children is the kind of time that will one day reap a great harvest. It is the time it takes to build the foundation on the rock and not on the sand. It is the time it takes to choose to keep one of these little ones God has blessed us with in the forefront of our daily activities while our favorite reality TV show, social networking site, or shopping endeavor will have to take a backseat for the moment.

# Chapter 4

# PATTERNS THAT
# UNDERMINE CHARACTER

S EVERAL YEARS BACK close friends of our family had invited us to their son's baby dedication service in the Rocky Mountain community of Estes Park, Colorado. It was a gorgeous autumn day for this memorable occasion. Everyone in the little mountain church anxiously awaited the dedication service to begin; my husband and I were seated a few rows from the front. The dedication began, but right at the most sacred and special moment, an exuberant fourteen-month-old, blonde-haired little girl popped up from the pew in front of us, completely blocking our view (and the view of those around us). All of a sudden all eyes were on this girl, not on the young boy who was being dedicated. The focal point, committing his precious life to the Lord, was lost. It was truly all about Little Miss Show Stealer in that moment. In the mind of this little girl she was supposed to be the center of attention, and she wasn't going to let anyone upstage her, especially not this baby! She was determined for all eyes to be on her.

We have all seen something similar: that child who is whining for candy at the checkout, the little boy who kicks his sister when he thinks no one is watching, the constant drama that surrounds our teens when they are at school or with their friends. I would not be overstating it to say that all of these situations manifest patterns of *iniquity*.

What is iniquity? This is where we need to deal with not only our children's manifestation of sin but also with the iniquity pattern that keeps the sin alive. The word *iniquity* is mentioned in the Bible more than 260 times, but most of us are not very familiar with it. The word comes from the Hebrew word *avah*, which means "to make crooked." Iniquity is the pattern that perpetuates sin. The literal meaning of the word *sin* is "to miss the mark." Let me use a word picture to explain the difference. Picture an archer shooting an arrow. Let's say he shoots and misses the mark, which we'll compare to sinning. But what was the cause of his missing the mark? What if the archer's shoulders were rotated to a position where they shouldn't have been, say by a mere four degrees? His position—the fact that he was standing in a crooked fashion when he shot the arrow—can be compared to iniquity. Lives bent by iniquity will always miss the mark.

Let us delve more deeply and take a look at how our children can operate either with the power of God that flows through them or the power of iniquity that causes them to miss the mark every time.

## LEARNING TO WALK STRAIGHT

The Bible says we need to separate "the precious from the vile" (Jer. 15:19, KJV), and that's what we need to do when dealing with our children and the power of iniquity in their lives. Parts of their lives have truly been crucified with Christ, and it is "no longer [they] who live but Christ who lives in [them]" (Gal. 2:20, NAS). Every one of our kids has the precious spirit part of them that has been cleansed by God and now functions in the power of the Holy Spirit. This is wonderful. But when we are trying to deal with the part of their lives that iniquity governs, that is the vile part. This is the part that needs to be put to death on the cross of Jesus Christ. It needs to be crucified and buried so that the life of Christ can arise within them. This is true not only for our children but also for everyone on the planet. If we are willing for this cleansing work of sanctification to take place in us, then we truly will be governed by the Lord Jesus Christ, and the power of a holy God will flow through us. We will be what the Bible calls a "living sacrifice" (Rom. 12:1), "dead" but with the power of God flowing through us.

Now this is not something that happens at a special service at church in which the power of God strikes us, we are moved, and we leave perfected. No, this happens as the result of an everyday, moment-by-moment surrender of little areas of our lives one by one as the Spirit of God gently (or sometimes not so gently) points them out to us to give up. This is part of our role as parents with our children. God has given us authority to root out these crooked places of iniquity in our children's lives.

Face it; when each of our kids landed in our laps on the day they were born, they arrived with all the strengths and gifts that God had given them. They also arrived with areas that, even fairly early on, God wants them to overcome. As our children grow day by day, we can see the specific areas of iniquity that they struggle with. If we dive in and help them begin to overcome these stumbling blocks while they are still young, they will not be left to wrestle with them for the rest of their lives. This is the incredible opportunity that we have as parents to be used by God to stand against the power of iniquity patterns that govern our kids' lives.

## INIQUITY PATTERNS

What are we looking for? I can see five patterns of iniquity in a single passage from the Bible:

> For you have said in your heart:
> "I will ascend into heaven,
> I will exalt my throne above the stars of
>     God;
> I will also sit on the mount of the
>     congregation
> On the farthest sides of the north;
> I will ascend above the heights of the
>     clouds,
> I will be like the Most High."
>                         —ISAIAH 14:13–14

Here is a modern-day application of how these principles of iniquity patterns work in our world today.

### The Chore Chart MVP ("I will ascend into heaven...")

This iniquity pattern causes a child to try to climb into heaven by his or her own works rather than by the grace of God. This child's desire to earn the esteemed most valuable player (MVP) award stems from the wrong motive. It does not come from a loving motive ("I want to help others") but instead from a selfish motive ("I want everyone to see how good I am.") Self-righteous, religious, "goody goody" children fall into this pattern. Wanting to appear as the best kid on the planet, this is the one who can never be wrong or get in trouble. At the core of this iniquity pattern is the lie "What I do (works) is more important than who I am."

### The Little Steam Engine ("I will exalt my throne above the stars of God...")

This is not "the little engine that could"; it's the little engine that you can't stop! These little people will stop at nothing to be the best. Competition is the arena they thrive in. The problem is that they are driven to flatten and level everyone in their path to get their way. They exalt themselves above others and will step on someone else to climb up their ladder of success. At the core of this iniquity pattern is the lie "I'm nothing if I'm not the best."

### The Aspiring Hollywood Star ("I will also sit on the mount of the congregation...")

This child is always at the center of everyone's attention. We have all seen it. This drive causes them to stop at nothing to be the focal point in every situation. Drama, drama, drama surrounds their every move and decision. The desire to be looked at, listened to, and given extreme recognition over every other child produces a whirlwind in any family or set of friends. At the core of this iniquity pattern is the lie "I deserve all the attention."

### The Never-Never Land Native ("I will ascend above the heights of the clouds...")

This child's modus operandi is checking out of reality. When anything seems difficult or challenging, he is the first one to go find another "world" to live in where life is easier and more controllable. This child would rather be playing a video game, reading a book, or lost in a movie than be a functional part of the family. He dwells in an alternate reality where everything has the perfect fairy tale ending. At the core of this iniquity pattern is the lie "This life is too hard, so I need to escape it."

### Unelected Dictator ("I will be like the Most High.")

This is the take-control child. The only problem is that these children are not just being responsible for themselves, they are demanding to control everyone in their environment as well! Are Mom and Dad allowed to be Command Central? No. Dominance and supremacy in this household has been self-bestowed on this preeminent one (and *not* because God or any other authority has declared it to be there!). At the core of this iniquity pattern is the lie "I, not God, can and must control every situation and the people in my life."

Now I have seen each and every one of these

iniquity patterns operate in my children at one time or another, but I have noticed that each child tends to major in one or two of them. It has been helpful for me to identify these patterns because those areas provide the mainspring for issues that we deal with over and over. When I can identify the iniquity motive behind their actions, it clarifies for them the areas they need to work on, especially as they get older.

## CONQUERING THE OLD NATURE

I love the classic story called *Teddy's Button*. This rare, old tale is a story about a young boy who moves to a new community after his father dies in battle. Written in the late 1800s, it still carries relevance for our lives today. The only earthly possession this young lad has to show for his relationship with his father is a button from his father's prized uniform.

The ups and downs of Teddy and his adventures to rid himself of his own strong-willed nature is a testimony for all of us.

At a young age Teddy decides to enlist in the "Captain's Army"—the army of the Lord. His wise pastor explains to Teddy the real enemy that he is fighting against. The pastor asks Teddy to close his eyes and then places him in front of a mirror. He tells Teddy to turn around on the count of three to see who the real enemy is. As Teddy turns around and sees his own reflection in the old mirror, he disappointedly exclaims, "'Aw. That's just me.'"

To which his wise pastor responds, "That's right, Teddy. You are your own worst enemy, and you will be fighting you for the rest of your life! Not only that—you will also be fighting others—with love."[1]

He then goes on to explain that while Teddy is serving the Lord Jesus, he will have two Teddys to deal with—the good Teddy and the bad Teddy. The pastor explains that we must fight against our old nature and gain territory by the blood of Jesus Christ.

After this is explained to him, Teddy understands that he has an old nature that gets him into all kinds of trouble. What I love about Teddy's adventure is that Teddy actually gave his old nature a name, "Bully." Then, determined to get rid of "Bully" and let the true "Teddy" shine through, Teddy separates the precious side of himself from the old, vile side whenever he is disciplined or corrected.

For many years my own children have done the same. At young ages they too gave their "self" a name such as Selfina, Toad, Ugly, and Stinky. They use these names to refer to their flesh, the part of their nature that Jesus Christ wants to crucify. This has been a tremendous help in our discipline. Our children have come to understand it is their flesh that needs discipline, but that we love and embrace the precious parts of them. This reassures them of our love and that we are dealing with only one aspect of their character. They are not "all bad" or "totally worthless."

They know that their "old man" needs to be crucified on the cross with Christ, because that is why Christ died for us, and that these places that are in each one of us need to conform to His image. They also understand that Mom and Dad love them so much that we are willing to tackle issues in their lives that keep them from becoming more like Christ. (See Romans 8:28–29.)

## REAPING AND SOWING

When one of the five iniquity patterns comes up in our children's lives, we need to help the child identify it and understand how sowing and reaping are involved in their choices. They need to understand that what they sow, they will reap. This is a very real principle. It is so real that God even arranges the consequences. As their parents we should arrange logical consequences when disciplining our children, but they need to know that even when we might not catch them in the act, God sees everything. A friend shared with me once that when she was eight years old, she stole some dimes. No one saw her, so she thought she got away with it, but later that week her brand-new bicycle was stolen from her. God impressed on her years later that the principle of sowing and reaping was involved.

So if your "Chore Chart MVP" is masking his or her motives with many "good works," you can be sure that God will arrange to expose that child. If you have a "Little Steam Engine" who is stepping on others to climb the social ladder at school, that child shouldn't be surprised to get stepped on or to fall into constant disagreements with friends. This lines up with Scripture: "And whoever exalts himself will be humbled, and he who humbles himself will be exalted" (Matt. 23:12).

The "Aspiring Hollywood Star" who lives at your house needs to understand that this iniquity drive to be the continual center of attention has its downside. God says in His Word that He will turn our idols/worshipers against us (Ezek. 23:22). It can be seen happening with every *People* magazine that we pass by as we check out at the grocery store. All the "worshipers" have turned against _____ (you fill in the latest and greatest name). Seriously, although our kids might never end up being the cover story on some tabloid, someone is always going to come along who outshines them. There will always be a bigger star that takes the limelight away from them. God just arranges it that way if they are determined to be worshiped.

True worship belongs to God alone, not to any of us.

The "Never-Never Land Native" cannot stay in never-never land forever, either. Sowing choices in this direction always reaps consequences that are arranged by God Himself, because God doesn't want us to live in a fantasy world. Sooner or later the young boy who uses video games to escape his difficult family or school situation will have his grades crashing around him because he never did his homework. The young teen girl who spends hours upon hours entertaining vain imaginations of herself as someone different will experience harsh reality playing its hand and drawing her up short. Although the dream world seems pleasant for the moment, in the long run it can lead to a nervous breakdown or mental illness.

"Unelected Dictators" are set on controlling their situation so they are the ones who come out on top every time. These are children who want to get their way—whatever it may take. Controlling and manipulating situations and people around them is vital. God will send someone to defeat them. Senseless wars have been fought because of these iniquities. In the end God always sees to it that these children will be defeated, not because He doesn't like them, but because He hates it when we walk in iniquity (Ps. 5:5).

## SURRENDERING INIQUITY

God is truly faithful to forgive us. Speaking for God, Jeremiah says it all:

> I will cleanse them from all their iniquity by which they have sinned against Me, and I will pardon all their iniquities by which they have sinned and by which they have transgressed against Me.
>
> —JEREMIAH 33:8

It will be valuable if you can help each of your children identify the iniquity pattern they operate in most, helping them see the way that this plays out in their everyday lives. Helping our children identify the lies that they believe and showing them how to replace them with the truth will set them free (John 8:32). This is often a process. Perfection does not come in a day. (Oh, how sometimes I wish it would!) Dying to self is a day-by-day, here-a-little, there-a-little process of being conformed to the image of His Son.

Iniquity patterns do not go away unless they are dealt with. Working with them now before your children leave home will help them grow into adults who walk in the ways of the Lord.

When my kids were in elementary school, we were well acquainted with a family whose daughter really struggled with being an "Unelected Dictator," especially when it came to her younger siblings. This was worsened by the fact that when the other kids were born, something inside her felt like she had been displaced as reigning queen, and she was determined to get that back. This played out in this family with lots of "mean girl" behavior. Now this sinful side of her was not blatantly obvious. (Many times this is the case with our kids' iniquity. We need the Holy Spirit to open our eyes to see what is really going on.) In her case there was also

> *Dying to self is a day-by-day, here-a-little, there-a-little process of being conformed to the image of His Son.*

enough of the "Chore Chart MVP" operating that the "good girl" image was all that many people could see. That happened consistently in situations where mean girl behavior was present. The mean girl knew how to impress those in authority around her so her mean behavior stayed under the surface and went unnoticed by authorities.

This girl's parents began to ask God to show them what was really going on. The Holy Spirit faithfully unraveled the motives and intentions of hearts and helped them to get to the depths of the situation. However, it was difficult to get through to her about it at first. The "Chore Chart MVP" part of her had not only convinced everyone else that she was the "perfect" child, but it had deceived their daughter as well.

With lots of truth being poured in, God brought into the light circumstances that showed her how she tried to control the other children and place herself as "mini god" in their lives. God began to remedy the situation by revealing how consistently she was the boss of the other children. When they would meet new friends, she made the ones she liked off-limits to her siblings; they were exclusively hers. If her sisters and brothers would dare to argue with her, it was an immediate losing battle for them. Not only was she trying to be god in their lives, but her sinful nature had accomplished dictatorship over the parents as well because her behavior was going on unnoticed by them. Her iniquity was ruling.

The "Little Steam Engine" pattern also came up in this family, because while this child could always be better than one of her sisters or brothers, her consistent message to them was that they were "nothing" and "couldn't do anything right." She would shrewdly cause her siblings to look bad in different situations. She would be playing a violin duet, and she would slyly bungle some notes, making it appear that her younger sister was lost and unable to play the piece. Their parents began to see that the younger siblings' self-esteem was subtly being undermined in a purposeful way by this other child as she tried to establish that she was "the best."

Sounds like an impossible mess, right? It would be if it weren't for God and His divine hand and favor. God is so faithful. If we will admit to ourselves we all have these "messy" dynamics in each of our families, God can intervene. God has placed each member of our families together because He wants to iron out some of these dynamics so that we can be conformed to the image of Jesus Christ. It *is* a mess—we are all a mess unless the Lord comes in and rescues us from ourselves with His redemptive hand!

Don't be discouraged when these iniquity patterns come up in your children. They are there, for sure. This is part of the journey that God has placed us on with our families so that out of a repentant heart we will worship Him with all our heart, all our soul, and all our strength (Deut. 6:5).

If we are willing to dive into our kids' patterns of iniquity, we will truly be discipling them. This is what parenting is about—walking with them, whether they are toddlers or teens, to bring these areas into submission to the Lord.

# Chapter 5

# PARENTS: THE GUARDIANS OF PURITY

FIGHTING FOR YOUR children's purity needs to begin young. I mean *really* young. Like right after your kids learn to walk. It is not something that you put on your checklist for the adolescence phase and think you have it covered. This is a constant battle, and if you did not engage your kids from the start, you have catching up to do.

To equip your children for the culture we live in, you need to have an age-appropriate course charted for each one. This plan needs to include how to talk to them about sex, future relationships, boundaries with technology, and the lies that sneak past us via the media. This plan is like a map. Before we had GPS devices, I had to get out the map and figure out how to get from point A to point B. Nowadays we have these fancy systems to help us. Personally, I don't trust them. Our GPS "person" (we named her Marsha) sometimes takes us the wrong way, so I still prefer to have a map as a backup.

Not only do you need to bring up a bunch of "dos and don'ts," but you also need to give your children a vision of what God has in store for them and build healthy convictions. God has an amazing love story planned for them, and it starts with falling deeply in love with Him. When our kids are very young, our relationship with them is a picture of their relationship with God their Father, God being their authority. Moms and dads, this is an opportunity to be a model of a healthy relationship with your child.

How pivotal it is to build convictions in our children and give them a vision for healthy relationships in the future! Just think about it: we spend an immense amount of time and money investing in our children's education and interests. We carefully choose the kind of schools that they will attend, whether public, chartered, private, or homeschool. We research the alternatives. We spend countless hours driving them to all the extracurricular activities that we have selected for them to participate in. We decide what sports they will compete in, what musical instruments they will learn, if they will be in drama or choir or both. But how much time do we invest in charting a course for their learning to build healthy relationships and strong character? How much time do we invest anchoring them in concepts such as purity of mind, heart, and body?

## LIFE LESSONS

Let's fast-forward a few years. After sending your son to the best schools and a prestigious university, let's say he is now thirty-five and married, with two kids and a dog. With diapers to buy, a mortgage to pay, and a high-stress job to go with it, his marriage hits the rocks. The fact that you picked the best schools and he was valedictorian, acing chemistry and calculus, will not come to his aid at this moment. What will be valuable to him at this point is what you taught him about how to have healthy relationships, strong communication skills, and conflict resolution know-how. His academics will not save his marriage (unless somewhere along the line he received a degree in family and marriage counseling). These are the life skills that are often overlooked as we invest in our kids.

We have their best at heart, and we desire for them to grow up and be successful, yet the foundation of what that takes has been skewed in a culture that prizes the wrong definition of success:

> For this world's wisdom is foolishness (absurdity and stupidity) with God, for it is written, He lays hold of the wise in their [own] craftiness; and again, the Lord knows the thoughts and reasonings of the [humanly] wise and recognizes how futile they are.
>
> —1 Corinthians 3:19–20, AMP

We need to equip our children not only with a strong academic education but also with a strong foundation of God's true wisdom. How much time do we spend intentionally teaching our kids these life lessons? We need to chart a course in this direction from the time our children are very young.

We also need to be sure that we are the ones to give the first message to our kids about sensitive topics such as sex, because the first message they hear is the most powerful. It needs to be from you, Mom and Dad, and not from the kid down the street or the kid at school.

One mom shared with me how her son's friends had enlightened him on how the sperm and the egg met. He told her what he had learned: that a boy must stick his penis into the girl (down there in that hole), and then after that the next step was that he would pee and it would then come out her nose. Now that is a word picture I have never forgotten!

I have heard hundreds of stories about how kids find out information on this subject, and, as humorous as they are, unless Mom and Dad are the source of information, it is usually misinformation that they are receiving. If we don't tell them, they will find out some way or another. Worse yet they may receive completely destructive information that could influence them to travel down a very dark path.

Just because they do not ask does not mean they do not want to know or that they do not already know. I had a mom come to me several years ago. She was convinced that her daughter was too young to know the facts about the birds and the bees, even though she was asking questions about where babies come from. The mom had given birth to this child out of wedlock before she became a Christian. Then she had come to Christ, met a wonderful man, and married him before her daughter was two years old. Together they had had more children.

In a roundabout way the daughter had asked her mom about how babies were made, but she had not received the full facts. Mom thought she was not old enough to hear the truth. But she was old enough to do the math. Soon she realized that her mom was not married yet at the time of her birth, and since she had never been told all the circumstances surrounding her birth, she decided that she was created by immaculate conception, just like Jesus!

Kids make all sorts of wrong assumptions when we parents decide we would rather leave a talk about sex until they are older. This is why the first message about where babies come from needs to come from us, preferably starting when they are around three (in a very age-appropriate fashion, of course).

Our children's hearts are very moldable at this young age, and we want to be the ones to make the first impression on them. We want to make sure that the truth of God is written on their young hearts. Several years ago the city came to repair a broken concrete slab in front of our house in Colorado. Now at this time we had a cat named Rover. This Rover was no ordinary tabby; he was at least twice the size of any normal cat and had twice the ornery personality to go along with his proportions. He was *always* attracted to trouble! Well, that day as they poured the new cement, I found him standing proudly out front, in the middle of that fresh concrete! At that moment I had visions of our tabby becoming a permanent part of our sidewalk! As I yelled for him to get in the house, he left his paw prints indelibly sunk into the brand-new cement. Even though Rover is long gone now, he is forever memorialized out in front of that home!

Our kids' hearts are the same way. They are like freshly poured cement when they are young, and this is our opportunity to instruct them about their character and to plant a vision of healthy future relationships and a deep love for the Lord. But do not think for a minute that we are doing all this without conflicting messages. There are a lot of "Rovers" out there in the world who know our kids' hearts can be written on at this age as well, and they want to get their "paws" on our children and scratch their ugly messages on their hearts.

We also do not want to wait too long before we start this process. If we wait too long, the cement will harden, and it will be like chipping rock to make these foundational messages stick. The sooner we are able to set these principles in our children's hearts, the sooner it will be set in a permanent way.

## TODAY'S PICTURE OF ROMANCE

Dramatic changes have transformed our culture over the past few years. The landscape has changed so drastically that it is safe to say that the world our kids are growing up in is not the same world that you and I used to know. One of the largest, most noticeable changes surrounds romance and relationships. There is no such thing as a soda fountain romance anymore! In fact, many kids have sworn off boyfriend/girlfriend relationships altogether in favor of "hooking up" for sexual encounters with "no strings attached."

The fact is, we need to begin fighting on behalf of this generation. We need to give them a vision for how God's love story for their lives was hand-crafted for each one of them. We need to tell them that He has an amazing, unique plan for each one of them. This generation is not seeing healthy, happy, whole marriages. Typically they don't see godly examples reflected on a consistent basis in the lives of those around them. Even if your immediate family is healthy and thriving, your children will see plenty of unhealthy, destructive examples, whether it is with their friends' families, your extended family, or through the media.

The concept of marriage cannot be conveyed merely with our words; it must be shown first in our actions. If our children do not see any proof of God's awesome plan in our marriage, they will be skeptical (at best) that a "God story" can happen to them. Our marriages need to reflect that this is an incredible, dynamic relationship that is *worth* waiting for. Otherwise our kids oftentimes decide to forgo marriage, opting for a live-in relationship or settling for one failing dating relationship after another.

Parents, you are your child's greatest example when it comes to relationships. The way they view dating and the opposite sex will largely come from your influence. Do you honor your spouse? Do you enjoy being around each other? Do you laugh together and show that marriage *is not* the end of love, affection, and romance?

Now, this isn't to say that if you have had marital difficulties or have suffered through a divorce that you are a failure as a parent and your child is doomed to a wrecked love life. On the contrary, this does not have to be true. But it is critical that you help your children still see the incredible plan God has for families and relationships, and that even if there have been some bumps in the road, He still has a love story to write for their lives. Come alongside your children and help them trust the Lord for their future spouse. Don't let a few setbacks forever alter their view of love, sex, and relationships.

## THE KEYS TO GUARDING

I see four different keys that are important for us to use as the guardians of purity for our children.

First, we have to be *intentional* with our children. We need to plan to talk about their purity of heart, mind, and body at every available opportunity and on a consistent basis.

Second, we need to be *purposeful*. This takes deliberate planning on our part. Every year we need to chart a course for what we are going to cover with them, just as we do with their academics. Remember, you wouldn't leave their mathematics or science to chance, so don't allow it with their training in virtues. I've written an age-by-age curriculum guide for preschool through eighth grade called *Against the Tide*.[1] It is a practical resource for parents to understand which resources to use at every age and stage.

Third, we need to be *protecting*. We need to set boundaries, with clear expectations and limitations in place. Our children need to know our expectations and what will happen if they choose not to abide by those expectations. Follow-through is incredibly important with boundaries. If you consistently promise a consequence (whether good or bad) to your child and that consequence is never delivered, then boundaries and expectations become fluid and determined by your child instead of you.

Fourth and last, we need to be *persevering* to keep boundaries in place when our kids push. They will all try to see if that line we have told them not to cross is adjustable or not. We need to persevere in our convictions when there is pressure to change to be like everybody else. Typical kids will push boundaries, especially in the area of friends, media (TV, movies, social networking, gaming), and relationships. Set up boundaries and stick to them, even when your kids push.

As your children get older, boundaries sometimes need to be adjusted to fit their ages and maturity level. Prayerfully consider these adjustments and make them based on God's direction, not manipulation from the children.

## KNOWLEDGE VS. EXPERIENCE

We need to be intentional and purposeful about giving our children every bit of knowledge that they need about future choices they are going to have to make. God did this with Adam and Eve in the garden. He gave them the knowledge they needed to succeed, and He told them clearly. And although Adam and Eve had the knowledge, they demanded to live by experience—just as in our day—eating from the tree of the knowledge of good and evil.

The truth is this: as much as we provide knowledge, some of our kids will demand to live by experience. Working with our children in an intentional and purposeful way is not a foolproof solution. Some of our children will choose to go around that mountain of less-than-ideal choices. But do not be discouraged. Keep equipping them with everything they need to fight the battle at hand. Just because they lose a few skirmishes does not mean that they have to lose the war.

If you have more than one child, do not give up being protecting and preserving just because one of your children demanded to live by experience and not knowledge. Each of our kids is so different. They all need to be empowered and equipped. I have watched many well-meaning parents, who are doing their best to equip their kids, throw in the towel when one of their children begins to make foolish choices. They conclude that the training they have done does not make any difference. But just because one child demands to live by experience rather than knowledge does not signify that all their efforts were amiss.

At one time or another we all have gone astray. We all need the grace and redemption of Christ. God has a way of taking hold of everyone's heart, and He knows what it will take even if one of our children is stubbornly determined to do his or her own will. It is crucial that we remain intentional and purposeful with each child, not letting one's unacceptable choices deter us from equipping our other children.

## TRUTH FROM THE WORD

Remember the line from the Lord's Prayer: "Lead us not into temptation, but deliver us from evil" (Matt. 6:13, KJV). Parents, don't allow your kids to flirt with evil. The intense pressure in our world today makes us want to give in and say, "Well, just a little bit of compromise is OK." The Word of God says, "Don't flirt with evil." Leaving a little room for the flesh creates a hunger and appetite that is not easily starved. Start off on the right foot, and don't compromise your standards when it comes to media, technology, and pure relationships.

Make certain that you are protecting what is going on inside your children as well as on the outside. Proverbs 4:23 (NLT) says "Guard your heart above all else, for it determines the course of your life." It really matters what is going on inside your kids' hearts and minds.

I have met so many teenagers who have their parents totally duped. It is not because they set out to be deceitful and hide their actions from their parents. They want to please their parents, but deceitfulness is required in order to maintain their parents' favor while acting in a way that is contrary to their family's standards. What goes on inside the heart always comes out in actions at some point. I love what Kris Vallotton says in his book *Moral Revolution: The Naked Truth About Sexual Purity*:

> [Y]our virtues train your attitudes, attitudes dictate your choices, choices decide your behavior, and your behavior

determines your destiny. The way that this whole process begins is by giving your virtues authority over your thoughts. If your virtues do not govern what you allow yourself to think about, this process of reaching your destiny will be sabotaged. Trying to behave inside your virtues, without taking control of what movie is being shown in the theater room of your heart, simply won't work. Everything in life begins with a thought, an image that is projected on the movie screen of your mind.[2]

Training your kids to guard their hearts is one of the most vital areas you will train them in. This is part of protecting their purity. Issues of life flow from the heart. Attitudes, choices, behaviors, and destiny are all at stake. Where is your child's mind dwelling? Have you ever checked? You need to dig deep and get in touch not only with their actions but what is happening on the inside as well. This is the arena where the battles are won and lost.

## TURNING BACK AT THE GATE

It is imperative to teach your kids to turn back the battle at the gate of their minds before it becomes a stronghold:

> He will be a spirit of justice
>     to him who sits in judgment,
> a source of strength

to those who turn back the battle at
the gate.
—Isaiah 28:6, niv

Media and society have exerted an extreme
amount of time, effort, and energy to blast their
own messages to our kids, so much so that it has
begun to "rewire" the way that this generation
thinks and understands. Twisted thinking and
ideologies have become "normal." But we are not
after normal, are we? We want to forgo ordinary
for the extraordinary. Let's equip our kids to guard
their minds against the messages of the enemy so
that he has no foothold in their lives and no way of
dragging them down his negative path.

If you have a teen, perseverance is a key ingre-
dient of your battle right now. The world advises
you that as parents, you don't really make a difference in the lives of your teens, so why bother
anyway? The world will try to tell you that your
teens will listen only to their peers and MTV, so
you might as well stop adding to the noise and
be quiet. But parents, let me assure you that this
is far from the truth! You have influence, impact,
and authority no matter what it feels like at this
present moment! Remember this truth, and keep
pressing onward! Persevere with the boundaries
that you have set in place. Keep it up, no matter
how much your heart is suffering over the choices

that your teens are making. Remember this truth from Scripture:

> Not only so, but we also rejoice in our sufferings, because we know that suffering produces perseverance; perseverance, character; and character, hope.
> —ROMANS 5:3-4, NIV

Sometimes you may feel as though you are suffering right along with your teens. The choices they make can be truly heart wrenching, and some days you feel like you have had all you can take. That is when you need to remember that God is using this stage in *their lives* to produce perseverance, character, and hope in *your lives* as parents. As I'm sure is true in your family, the Lord uses my kids for my growth in Him every single day.

Your perseverance with your children is what produces character in them. As you kneel at God's almighty throne and open your heart, God will show you what is necessary for that child who is causing you fits right now. He is faithful to instruct you in your parenting for each and every unique situation that you encounter. That is why spending time by His side is your most

*Let's equip our kids to guard their minds against the messages of the enemy so that he has no foothold in their lives and no way of dragging them down his negative path.*

valuable asset in raising the next generation. Only in His presence will we find hope for the next generation.

Parenting through these stages is not about following a rigid formula someone has come up with; it means seeking God with all your heart and hearing from the Lord about the next step He would have you take with your child. Every child is unique and requires a unique response.

Urge your children to hear from God, and you do the same as well. I believe that God is speaking the same thing to both our children and us. He is faithful and will not lead us astray. I cannot stress enough that there is no recipe for parenting except to be on our knees before the throne of God, first and foremost. This is the first step. Then God will lead us to the place where we will find the answer for each child.

## Chapter 6

# BUILDING CHARACTER
# THAT LASTS A LIFETIME

THERE ARE WHOLE books written for parents about how to build character in their kids. Some of us have such books—sometimes advocating conflicting philosophies—on every bookshelf in our homes. As a new mom I remember trying to get my child to sleep through the night. I found a book that advised, "Let them scream it out," and the next book I looked at told me the exact opposite—to snuggle the child in bed with me! Every new bit of "expert" advice was the complete opposite of the previous one! How are we to know what to do?

With each of our children being so unique, we

need to hear from God for each child in each situation. God knows the answer to everything we face with each one of our children, and when we get down on our knees before Him, He is not going to leave us without grace and wisdom. Having said that, let me tell you that the carpet next to my bed is worn thin! There is nothing that gets me on my face before God like my family.

It is so important to learn to hear God's voice moment by moment as we seek to build a strong foundation of character. Shaping begins in our children's hearts. We don't want to raise a generation that can do all the right actions on the outside but without the right heart on the inside.

How can we pull back the curtain and look at what is going on with our children's thoughts, motives, and intentions? Take a journey with me to look deeper at the inside and not just the outside.

## TAKE A GOOD LOOK

Just because we raise our kids in a Christian home does not mean that they are immune to the grip of this culture. Sending them to youth group does not save them from sin. The challenge for us as parents is that we want to believe the best when it comes to our kids. We would like to only focus on the good things that are manifesting in their lives and character. (Face it; this makes us look good as parents!) In the same way, especially as our kids get older, they want us to be proud of them. They will go to great lengths to cover situations that need correction because they want us to see the positive things they are doing. Parents and children have been doing this for generations. Take a look at the Bible: Adam and Eve, David, Jacob—just to name a few.

In order to achieve a balanced approach to building our kids' character, we parents need to look honestly at both their strengths and weaknesses. I know most parents reading this chapter feel that they do that, but in ministering to thousands of parents, I have found it to be a big obstacle.

Ask God right now to reveal to you the thoughts, motives, and intentions of each of your children by name at this moment. This is how God's Spirit desires to do the deep work in all of our hearts, especially the hearts of our kids.

As we started doing this in our church fellowship, the Holy Spirit began to unearth some pretty serious stuff. Now some of us back away from this work because we don't want to face all the messes that spill out as we deal with the stones in our kids' hearts. Our kids are just like adults; they are experts when it comes to covering sin. I have witnessed countless situations where kids successfully play the "good Christian" while what is going on inside did not match up with the rest of the act.

One girl I know had successfully hidden deep ongoing sin for almost ten years. Although you would never have known it from the outside, she was obsessed with sex. On the outside she was a perfect Christian girl. She did and said all the right things. She was modest and polite, and she served in the church. But hidden in darkness, in the secret places in her heart, sin had manifested itself, and it had become a serious problem. It started with watching movies and reading books with inappropriate content when she was about eleven years old. It seems that many of us have movies on the shelves that require us to fast-forward through that one scene. Well, she would take those movies and watch those scenes on the DVD player in her room in the middle of the night. With each viewing, the stronghold became more and more entrenched.

After ten years of it, a time came when God positioned her in a corner, and she broke down and confessed. As she looked back over the sin that had entrapped her, she realized that it all started out as one little lie. She believed the lie that what she did in secret would not impact her life as long as no one found out. Believing and walking in lies can alter the course of our lives and take us off God's chosen path. The lies inside destroy you. As this young woman said after God had begun His work with her, "Who you are on the inside is going to matter more than who you are on the outside."

Things go on in secret in our kids' lives. How do we know it? First of all we have to be willing to face it. Admit it; we are threatened when our kids are not perfect. We look around on Sunday morning and seem to be surrounded by all these "perfect" families that look like they have it way more together than we do. This is a lie perpetuated by the enemy. It seems like we all strive to live the "normal" Christian life. The fact is, there is no family that does not have issues. A dear intercessor friend of mine always says, "Normal is a setting on the dryer. Other than that, there isn't any normal!" It's so true; we are always looking to be "normal" and have some measuring stick to compare ourselves with. We need to get over it. Everyone around us has issues. Their kids have issues. No one is as perfect as they make themselves out to be!

Just because it seems as though your family does not have it all together does not mean that you are a failure or that God doesn't take care of you. If you adopt this perspective, you will never be willing to deal with the hard stuff. God does not view it this way. If we had it all together, why would we need His Son to die on the cross for our sin? God sees our hearts and accepts and loves us no matter what He sees. Are we willing to do that with our own children?

This is an issue of being willing to mentor and disciple your kids through all their struggles. Kids make choices. You are not responsible for the choices they make, but you are responsible, as God directs you, to disciple them with consequences through these choices. Better to catch the stones in your kids' hearts now while they are still young. If you walk with them through it now, they will not have to live with it the rest of their adult lives where there are more serious consequences for sin. Set patterns of freedom and not bondage in your kids' lives. Be willing with open arms to lovingly walk them through issues and patterns that need to be broken. I urge you not to turn a blind eye simply in order to feel acceptable to them or to those surrounding you.

Many parents ask me, especially if they have teens, how they can know the hidden things in their hearts. First, pray that God will show you the thoughts, motives, and intentions of their hearts. Next, if they are spending significant periods of time alone and are vague about what they are doing, this is a clue that something may be going on, especially when teens spend chunks of time behind closed doors. If your teen is locking the door to his or her room, that should be a hint to you.

I like what Ronald Reagan said: "Trust everyone; verify everything."

Teens use technology to hide their sin. Teens are no longer young enough so that you can block their every move with filters, but you can still help them learn how to use technology responsibly and to be above reproach. Monitoring software is an effective way to do this.

The essential point for us as parents is that we are willing to confront these issues with our children. We can't let our own iniquity patterns of not wanting to face the difficult realities of situations (being like the Never-Never Land Native) or wanting to appear perfect (like the Chore Chart MVP) get in the way of helping our kids grow to their full potential and destiny in the Lord.

## DIGGING THE FOUNDATION: THE WORD OF GOD

When your kids are toddlers, in preschool, and in elementary school, this is your opportunity to get the Word of God into their moldable little hearts. Take every opportunity to plant the seeds of the Word. Remember it will not return void:

> So shall My word be that goes forth from My mouth; it shall not return to Me void, but it shall accomplish what I please, and

> it shall prosper in the thing for which I
> sent it.
>
> —ISAIAH 55:11

Read the Word of God all the time, and have your children listening to the Word. As a family during our family devotion times, we have spent time together listening to the Bible. One year we decided to embark on listening to the Bible in a year. Many people read the Bible in a year, but we decided that we were going to listen to it together as a family. We would sign on to a Bible website where they had an audio version of the Bible. Now because sometimes things would come up during devotions and we would skip time here and there, we are still trying to get through the year of listening! The important thing, I figure, is that we are doing it no matter how long it takes. We want to lay the foundation of our kids' lives on the Word of God, so they have a love for His Word in them.

Encourage your kids to be creative about diving into God's Word. When our daughter Hana was only four years old, she took a blank journal and started illustrating her own Bible. She started with Creation and drew pictures all the way through the Old and New Testament. It amazed me how many stories were included in her book. She of course got all the major ones, but she also included the ones that we as adults often don't consider (for instance, the story of the captured Jewish servant girl and her master, Naaman the leper, from 2 Kings 5). Any way that our kids can connect with God through His Word is good, and it will be foundational to their character development.

Also, taking time to memorize Scripture with our children will bear much fruit in the coming years. Take different key verses or memorize a chapter at a time with the whole family. Challenge each other to store God's Word in your heart.

As we discussed before, each one of our children comes in with weaknesses to overcome. I would encourage you to use Scripture to counteract these behaviors. For instance, maybe you have a "Chore Chart MVP" in your house. Scriptures that focus on pride and self-righteousness will be very helpful for that child to memorize. The truth of God's Word does not condemn, but through it our struggles and strongholds can be broken.

Like so many places in the world, we take for granted the fact that the Word of God will be there, right at our fingertips, any time we want it. Years ago a dear friend was ministering in a country that was closed to the gospel. He assisted in smuggling in Bibles and was meeting with some of the underground church leaders. At one meeting an elderly woman in her late seventies walked up to him and asked him for a Bible. He responded to her request by asking her if this Bible was for her or someone else. The reply he got back startled and surprised him. She said, "No, our village already has a Bible. This Bible is for the next village near us. I have walked for three days to come to you to get this Bible for them." As he thought of all the Bibles we have just sitting on our shelves at home, his heart was pierced with conviction and thankfulness that we can so freely have the Word of God in our possession.

## OBEDIENCE

One time when we were on a family ministry trip in Southeast Asia, we took a few days at the end of the trip for some rest and relaxation. Since we had just been ministering in Jakarta, Indonesia, we went to Bali for a few days. One day my kids were playing in the swimming pool at the resort (it was a very nice resort, five-star all the way), and they were going down the slide in the kiddie pool. Now I had assumed that, at a resort of this caliber, the children's pool would be a safe environment for our children. Well, as I was watching my seven-year-old get ready to go down the slide, I looked down, and all of a sudden I saw three giant iguanas in the pool! I guess they had wandered in and the resort staff had not caught on yet. There was my daughter ready to come down the slide and these fierce-looking animals were at the base of the slide! As calmly as a mother could,

I told her not to proceed down the slide. If she had not been obedient the first time I asked, I'm sure that she would have just gone right on down and landed in the pool with three child-eating dragons! (OK, I'm not positive that they eat children, but they looked as if they could!) Thankfully she obeyed right away.

We backed her down the stairs and avoided the kids' pool from that time onward. While your children may not be threatened by a man-eating dragon (hopefully our family will also manage to avoid them in the future!), there is a deeper purpose to this story. I share this story with you to emphasize the importance of obedience. For every family in every nation there will be times when obedience is absolutely critical. These are the times that obedience matters the most.

I pray that my children learn obedience—not only obedience to my husband and me, but first and foremost to God. We need to teach our kids that the person they are when no one is watching is when their character speaks loudest. I always pray that God will bring into the light the times when their disobedience is hidden from me. God has a way, it seems, of catching our kids in the act, because He wants them to learn from their choices and the consequences of their choices. So many times one of my girls will think that no one will catch her when she is doing something, but God allows one of us to see it. He wants her heart—a heart that is freely willing to obey.

Our neighbors once shared a story with us about a babysitter whom they had hired to watch their grandchildren while they all went out for a nice dinner together. They were thoroughly enjoying their time away, and also the great babysitter that they had landed from church. This seemingly nice, innocent, sixteen-year-old girl was a rare find! But things are not always what they seem.

> We need to teach our kids that the person they are when no one is watching is when their character speaks loudest.

As it turned out, after this young lady had put the children to bed, she jumped on the home-owner's computer and began surfing pornographic websites. But what this young girl didn't know was that the homeowner had accountability software installed on his computer because he believed in living a life above reproach. This accountability software required him to have an accountability partner, and this man had chosen his pastor.

So midway through dinner this gentleman got a call from his pastor, asking why in the world he was visiting porn sites! Of course, the man reassured him that he was not even at home, and the next realization was that the only one home, the sixteen-year-old girl, must have been the one on the computer. She never imagined that she would be caught.

So many times our kids think that they have gotten away with something because they wrongly assume that no one is watching. But God is always watching and arranging circumstances of sowing and reaping so that He can deal with their character.

Our children need to understand that obedience can literally save their lives. It starts with learning obedience to us as parents when they are young, because this is the way they learn to be obedient to God their Father ultimately. The Word tells us: "If you [really] love Me, you will keep (obey) My commands" (John 14:15, AMP). Love and obedience to the Lord should be at the heart of their motivation.

When our kids walk out the door on their way to adulthood, I want them to know and understand obedience to God and, most importantly, to do it. We parents are not always going to be looking over their shoulders when they get to college to tell them to do this or that. No, by that point they should have had years of practice hearing the still small voice of the Holy Spirit instructing them in obedience to Him. When adulthood comes, the best way that they can honor us as parents is to hear the voice of the Lord and obey it. It is no longer about doing their parents' will but about doing the will of God.

## MANNERS

Good manners are foundational to good character. We need to focus on manners, not only when our kids are young but also especially as they enter their tween years. This will help our boys, especially, to win their future battle for purity, because learning common courtesy and understanding how to respond as a gentleman will instill in them how to show respect for the young ladies around them. Good manners will also ground them in servanthood, and the basis of servanthood is self-denial. In the future being able to deny themselves and not just to plow ahead to get what they want will prove to be foundational to a healthy sense of self.

Manners come and go at our house. This gives us opportunities to consistently brush up on them. Sometimes for a season we read books about manners; the one our family has enjoyed most is called *Everyday Graces*.[1] The editor has creatively addressed manners through a collection of poems, short stories, and excerpts from chapter books. This book makes learning about manners as fun as reading an entertaining story, and reading a bit at the table each day at lunch or dinner has been fun to do.

At different times we also have held a "manners

week" in which we do a crash course in table manners and other kinds of manners.[2] We put a list on the table of manners that we are going to work on and make a monumental push to get them engrained in our children in that week (sometimes this takes more than one week!).

Also, having a date night with each of your kids is a great way to introduce manners training. When Mom takes her son on a date, she gives the young man a chance to practice holding the door open, learning how to treat a woman at a restaurant, and even paying the bill (well, Dad might have to quietly subsidize that one!). When dads take the time to take their daughters on dates, the way that their father treats them is how these precious young girls will expect to be treated by men in the future.

The point is we want to teach our children that other people are worth caring for—which is essentially what practicing good manners does. It says, "I care about you, so I am going to control my behavior so you will feel comfortable and well taken care of." We express this principle whenever we look people in the eye in conversation, remain mindful of things we say in their presence, hold the door for them, or tell them "thank you." Manners training teaches them valuable principles such as self-control and compassion. Manners training teaches me as a child that there are other people in the world—people who are affected by *my* behavior.

If our kids can make the connection between their behavior and how it affects other people, they will be more likely to abstain from sexual promiscuity. They will have ample practice in self-control and sacrifice. Every time they forgo the last cookie in the box so their younger sibling can have it, they are practicing. When your son learns it's not appropriate to spit in front of Grandma, he is learning something significant about the differences in sensibilities between men and women.

These are the implicit lessons we teach our children. Now, please don't misunderstand the message here. Manners training is just a part of the whole training when it comes to purity. Our kids need the implicit messages about respecting other people as well as the outright, clear messages about respecting God-given sexual boundaries. We can't do one and not the other; they need both. (For those of you panicking about giving "the talk," don't worry. We'll get to that in another chapter.)

Especially in the "tween" years stage, it would be easier to overlook poor manners. This is often-times when slang terms and four-letter words sneak into your child's vocabulary. I would encourage you not to let these things go unaddressed nor to pass them off as a phase or "normal" behavior. It is important that we express what is or isn't acceptable in this area. We want their consciences still to be pricked and soft when they do something that they *know* goes against our values.

As we go through the ups and downs on character training, remember, parents: God has your back on this one! Do not lose heart as you're working with your children and things come into the light. Realize that this is ultimately for their freedom and benefit. The enemy would like to discourage you and bring you down when you see your children making less-than-positive choices. But do not let that dampen your spirits. Keep forging ahead to lay a strong foundation of character and virtue in the lives of your children. You are laying a foundation that a pure generation can be raised upon!

# Chapter 7

# DEVELOPING PURITY
# MUSCLES

I F YOU'RE ANYTHING like me and have ever made a resolution to get in shape, you know that getting into shape and being in shape are two different ends of the continuum. I go out the first day all enthusiastic, ready to do the amazing workout, giving it my all; only to wake up the next morning so sore that I am not able to get out of bed! But if I am able to keep this workout schedule over time, soon I get stronger, and I am not in pain every day. My muscles are able to handle more and more.

"Purity muscles" are like that too. The character of our kids needs to be strengthened to give them the incredible fortitude and strength they are going to need to stand strong against the godless principles of our culture today. For their sakes we should have a "purity workout schedule" in place while they are growing up.

We need to learn to work the different "muscle groups" in our children's purity regimen. There are many ways that we can prepare our children for the future while they are yet naïve. This basic undergirding will enhance their ability to stand against the tide of culture when they reach adolescence. Intentional planning on our part will strengthen them to stand in the future.

## An Image That Reflects God's Design

From the time your kids are very young, you must build strength into their self-image, gender, and body image. Let your children know how beautiful and handsome they are. This is critical in a culture that starts telling children when they're young that they do not look right. Dads, on a regular basis remind your daughters how lovely God made them. The campaign that is expressly designed to negate our daughters' self-image starts very early. Advertising is a major culprit in undermining their opinion about their outward image and appearance.

Teach your children early on that God knew perfectly well what He was doing by making a little girl or a little boy. We want to make an ongoing effort to build our children's confidence in their gender. When you see your child acting in a way that affirms his or her gender, you can use it as an opportunity to validate God's amazing design for that child's life.

When you see your daughter all dressed up as a princess and having a tea party, you might interject, "Isn't it wonderful that God made you such a beautiful little girl?" Or when you see your son dressed up as a pirate and climbing a tree, pretending it is the mast on a ship, you could say, "Isn't it great that God made you such an adventuresome little boy?" Now, it goes without saying that many little girls climb trees and little boys love to have tea parties with their moms, but we can still affirm them as God made them. When you catch your children doing an activity that affirms their gender, by all means point it out periodically. The gender, agenda starts young, and we need to arm our kids with an assurance that God the Creator knew what He was doing when he made each and every one of them.

So what do you do if you have a daughter who is a tomboy or a son who is sensitive and not as rugged as those around him? Again, it is vital to look at the motivation of the heart. I can remember one little girl I met who could definitely hold her own with the boys. She was determined to be just as good as they were at everything that she set out to do with them. Over time, talking with her, she could see that she had decided at some point that boys had it better than girls. In her mind boys got all the breaks. She had developed an inner determination not to be the girl God designed her to be. She didn't like being a girl because of this little, tiny lie in her that believed God made boys better than girls.

Little lies like this one can be woven into our kids' hearts and minds, and they make a huge impact on their choices and experiences as they grow older. When she started to see that God cherished her just as much as the boys and that He had an extraordinary plan for her life and future, her heart shifted, and she no longer felt God had made her something less. She still could compete with the boys, but there was a deep appreciation and joy over who God had designed her to be.

*God has made boys and girls so distinct, but the world is endlessly trying to muddle the differences.*

God has made boys and girls so distinct, but the world is endlessly trying to muddle the differences. Now boys seem to be hammered in this area even more than girls. I have seen boys struggle especially hard when they have failed to see a balanced model of a man. In a society where more than 25 percent of parents are single[1] (the overwhelming majority being single moms), this struggle is amplified. When boys are raised by a single mom, they are usually surrounded by caring, gentle, sensitive, supportive, and loving women, but no men. In some cases they have a completely contradictory model of a man who is extremely aggressive, selfish, vulgar, and dominating. This is an open door for the enemy to plant lie after lie about masculinity.

We need to look for a balance of healthy male and female traits. Even if a masculine role model is absent, Jesus can be your son's model of perfect balance in a man. Be sure to support your son when the enemy is undermining him, starting when he is young. Helping both sons and daughters grasp the blessing of being who God designed them to be is part of your job as a parent.

## THE MODESTY FACTOR

It's all so easy when your girls are young. Pretty dresses, cute little outfits, an abundance of lovely selections in the stores...and then it happens: They grow out of size 6X. Suddenly the clothing racks look as though they were transported in off the set of the latest teen girl band. Personally, I do not want to dress my girls like the latest rock star. It takes work to find clothes that are appropriate for your girls and that keep them looking their age. But let me tell you, it is worth it!

Parents face a battle as their girls get older in

what they should or should not wear. It is important to establish early (by the preschool years) what is and is not acceptable to wear. Take the opportunity to make these decisions when your girls are very little; don't wait until it becomes an issue. At this point decide how short is too short, what kind of swimsuits are acceptable, and how low and high everything can go. Then keep these standards consistent through the years.

Many families do not decide this early enough. Let me paint a picture of what happens as a result. Picture your fourteen-year-old daughter—beautiful, tall, just got her braces off, and looks like she's eighteen—when she walks out the door in the latest style of string bikini. What does it look like? Let's just say that this swimsuit has very little fabric on it. Dad, you stare in disbelief and sternly call her back into the house. You are worried that some twenty-five-year-old creeper is going to pick her up on the way to the beach! You proceed to tell her to go put on something more appropriate (i.e., something with more fabric). She is angry and feels rejected by you. This gives her an opportunity to believe the enemy's lie to her that tells her she does not look right.

Now you as the parent know that your daughter looks beautiful and amazing, in fact, so much so that a lot of men out there might get the wrong impression. The best way to keep this scenario from happening is to establish consistent standards from the time she is young through all the years of her growing up. Then your girls will not take your comments about modesty as grounds to be down on their own body image.

If you have a teen with whom you did not do this while they were younger and you now need to reconfigure your standards a bit, I suggest Dannah Gresh's book *Secret Keeper.*[2] This is a great little book, designed for teens, all about modesty and the power of true beauty.

## EVERYDAY ENDURANCE

Purity muscles must be built day by day, experience by experience. This muscle building is part of learning to stand strong. As parents we can make our kids' journeys much easier by keeping tabs on different challenges they face. For instance, it's important to know what goes on at other homes when we send our kids over to play. Especially when our kids have overnights with friends, we need to know what environment we are sending them into. What are the parents' standards in that home? If it is a family from church, do we just assume it is OK because we have seen them sitting in the pews on any given Sunday? What kinds of media and movies do they allow in their home?

I have had many teens tell me that their standards were challenged when they went to a good friend's home for an overnight. These kids share that they felt pressured into watching something on the big screen or Internet or played a game that compromised their standards. We need to have a system in place not only to communicate our expectations clearly but also to help our kids follow through.

If they are embarrassed and their purity muscles are not quite strong enough to just leave an uncomfortable situation, give them a code word they can tell you on the phone. This has worked well with our younger children as well as our older ones. The child can say something like, "Did Aunt Betty arrive from Colorado yet?" And since "Aunt Betty" doesn't usually visit at all because there is no "Aunt Betty," this would be your cue to answer, "Yes, we will be over to pick you up." Aunt Betty does not represent a person; in this instance, she symbolizes a cry for help.

This is not the same world that most of us grew up in. We used to have such freedom. I remember riding my bike all over town. In today's world we have to come to terms that there are very few places where it is safe to have this type of freedom anymore. We are called by God to protect our children, and that means we have to come to terms with the fact that this world is not safe. There are many out there who will take advantage of even a little child to satisfy their own selfish desire.

We also have to understand each family has different standards. God will help you design the standards for your home as you seek Him. Someday you will stand before Him, and He will hold you accountable for how you raised your children. You will not be able to blame their teachers, nannies, day-care workers, youth pastor, or others for how they were raised. God gave them to us; therefore we are accountable for their upbringing.

Situations that test your standards can come up at any time. We were at a Christmas party of a family in the neighborhood one year when our kids were young. The kids at the party were all in the basement playing games and watching a Christmas movie. My husband and I were perusing the goodies and chatting with neighbors when all of our kids came rushing up the stairs, exclaiming that the movie in the basement was completely inappropriate for kids! Someone had changed the movie to a selection that was really appropriate only for adults. They knew what our standards were, and they did not want to expose themselves to the content that was being shown.

Although we need to teach our kids to be tactful at these moments, it is more important that they know where they stand when it comes to making purity choices. Doing it creates strong purity muscles. Monitoring should not come only from parents and those around them but also from an internal compass that we must establish over time within our children.

## GARBAGE IN, GARBAGE OUT

Making choices when it comes to what our kids read and listen to is important as well. As soon as our kids are good enough readers to immerse themselves in the world of chapter books, the challenges start coming.

Reading is one of the absolute best ways our kids can enlarge their world. It is a gift when they enjoy reading and become avid readers. Reading is something we want to encourage in our children. While there is a world of excellent literature out there that has been written over time, there is also a lot of trash. My husband and I have come up with standards in the literature arena as well.

Now, our kids love reading, and sometimes it can be difficult to keep up with all that they want to read. Especially before they are teens they can be undiscerning in the kinds of books they pick up off the shelf at the bookstore or library. If you have been to the library lately, you will have seen countless books with objectionable content that centers around witchcraft, the demonic, and the sensual. No parent has enough time to assess them all. To solve this problem, we hired a young teen at one point to review books before we gave them to my younger kids. I helped my kids find books that looked appropriate. I then asked the teen to read it and look for any witchcraft, demonic content, romance, or other influences not in line with the Word of God. I paid the teen a few dollars a book to review it. The teen loved the job, and I loved that I got great book reviews!

Listening to music is another problem area, and we have to keep tabs on our children after their interest kicks into gear, usually when they are approaching their teen years. You need to know the words of the music that they are listening to. Countless teens have told me that they just like "the beat" and that they don't listen to the words, but music has a unique effect on our brains. Music that is heard over and over locks itself into a memory pattern that is very strong. If I started singing a popular tune from when you and I were in high school, we would be able to recall the words much more easily than we can recall other memories. Why? It is because the way our brains process music with words is very powerful. If the music your kids are listening to is not supporting the truth of Scripture, then it can undo many of the positive, godly messages that you have been sowing in their lives.

Consider this common music scenario: Good Christian kids stumble upon a popular, secular radio station online. (Yes, all radio stations are now online, free to listen to anytime, anywhere.)

Then they search for a way to listen to that catchy, new song without their parents finding out, since the lyrics and the artist are not appropriate. They find an illegal downloading site (or a legal site such as iTunes) and download the song. Then, in order to conceal the songs that they are listening to, they cleverly change the file names of the songs to be "parent-friendly." So, for instance, when Mom or Dad looks at the music list on the computer, the song title reads something Christian such as "Jesus Saves" when really it is "Sex on Fire." And when Mom asks, "Son, what are you listening to?" he proudly holds up his music gadget and exclaims, "See, Mom, I'm listening to 'Jesus Saves'!" when really, he is listening to a very trashy song. I wish I could say that this is an uncommon issue, but unfortunately that is far from the truth.

As parents we have our work cut out for us when it comes to music. Here are some practical things that you can do to stay on top of the trends:

- Keep track of what your kids are purchasing online. You can do this by having your credit card on their music purchasing account (such as iTunes). But more effectively, use your filtering and monitoring software to check where your kids are listening online.

- Especially for your young kids, if they come home saying they want to purchase a certain song, take a moment to look up the lyrics online. Are they appropriate? What about the artist? Is the person trashy or a good example?

- Use a dock or speakers for the music device instead of earphones. Even if it drives you nuts to have the music on, at least you know what they are listening to and what they enjoy!

- Music is a great way to connect with your kids; it is so influential to them. Take time to get to know the music they enjoy, and do some research. If their music choices aren't in line with your family values, give your kids different listening options. There are so many fantastic Christian bands these days that sing popular music with a positive message.

## WHY THESE MUSCLES NEED TO BE STRONG

Parents who help their kids build strong purity muscles are the parents who are not afraid to talk to their kids about sex. We need to present the facts to our kids in an age-appropriate fashion starting when they are young. We will talk about how to do this in the next chapter, but at this point I want to stress the importance of why we need to do this. I meet parents all the time who are reluctant to talk with their children. Many parents fall into this category. Face it: we are all nervous when it comes to sharing about all these sensitive issues. Maybe our parents never said anything to us, or maybe we have serious regrets in this area. But this generation needs to know about it and be equipped to fight this battle.

Over the years speaking to parents, I have found that in a room of four hundred parents, only a handful will raise their hands when I ask if their parents spoke to them about the birds and the bees. The younger these parents are, the higher the probability that their parents talked to them on a regular basis about these sensitive issues.

One day at a conference a mom came up and shared with me a tragic story. She told me about her thirteen-year-old son. Apparently Dad had been too busy to take him on the weekend they had been planning to share about the birds and the bees. Everyone knows how that happens; the urgent takes the place of the important. Well, she noticed that something had been bothering her son for well over a week. He was sullen and withdrawn. Then one night he finally came into her bedroom in tears and began to confess an event that had transpired a couple weeks before.

Keep in mind that this family had high standards, and they had encouraged their son to have very high standards as well. They had encouraged him to wait to kiss his wife on his wedding day. Although they had repeatedly shared this one statement with him, they had never gone beyond that. That night he shared that he had been at the park with a group of friends and they had begun to play a game of truth or dare. Well, one dare led to another, and by the end of everything he had ended up having sex with one of the girls. While confessing the entire event to his mom, he made the point that with everything that had transpired, he never kissed the girl, because of their clear expectation never to do that until he got married. Now if ever there was a time that the point of the matter was missed completely, I would say this was one of those times!

We need to give our kids clear guidance. We need to give them the entire picture. When we communicate clear expectations and set boundaries for our kids, they need all the pertinent information to work with. To have strong purity muscles, our children need to know what they are standing for and what they are standing against.

## FIT AND READY

Another "muscle group" that needs to be built up has to do with serving others. Isaiah wrote: "But the noble, openhearted, and liberal man devises noble things; and he stands for what is noble, openhearted, and generous" (Isa. 32:8, AMP).

Fortifying this muscle group in our homes is easy to do every day. We should be able to find plenty of opportunity right in front of us for teaching our kids how to be noble and servants, and this kind of character-building goes a long way. Later, when it comes to making hard choices about their purity of heart, mind, and body, children who can deny themselves and choose to honor others have an instant advantage.

We must teach our kids while they're still at home how to love others wholeheartedly and make personal sacrifices, instead of leaning on the perks of our prosperous culture, which can shelter our kids from lifting a finger to help. Many families have instant meals, someone who comes in to clean on a regular basis, a gardener, and a plowman who removes the snow that piles up in the driveway. Although this isn't bad, we need to make room for our kids to lay down their own agendas and be part of sharing the load as a member of the family. In preparing them for the future, we are preparing them not only to succeed academically but also how to run a household successfully. Our homes are the perfect training ground for our children to grow up with everything they need to be successful adults.

Of course, the deeper significance of their doing chores diligently is that they are learning to sacrifice their own agendas as well. They will not be able to learn this if we parents provide them with too much of "the good life," to the degree that we cause our kids to miss out on the responsibilities that are necessary for their growth.

Granted, it can be a real challenge for us to get them to follow through on their household duties on a regular basis, so we just cave in because it is easier to do it ourselves, or we hire it out to someone else. This kind of training is certainly a time investment, but without it our kids cannot grow up into responsible adults who can love others wholeheartedly.

## CONFLICT RESOLUTION

Right in the midst of our home life we find another vital element of training that often goes unnoticed—learning to get along with siblings. When I speak, I always ask young people to raise their hands if they have a brother or a sister. A good percentage of the hands are raised in the audience. Then I ask them if they ever argue or squabble with their siblings. Again, hands are up all over the room. This, I say, is the gift God has given them to learn how to communicate effectively and resolve conflict. If they learn to do this now, they will have the skill of communication and conflict resolution when they are married.

Here's how this works at our home. One night my husband and I put the kids to bed and we were relaxing downstairs and finishing up the day's work. All of a sudden we heard screams coming from our daughters' room upstairs. We both charged upstairs, wondering what on earth was up. Bursting into the bedroom, we found both girls crying and holding their heads. (They were five and seven years old at the time.) Upon looking closer, we could see that our younger daughter was not really crying and had stopped holding her head. So there went the bumping-heads theory. (I had assumed that one was hanging down from her bunk and had bumped the other one.) So I asked my younger daughter what happened. Without hesitation she explained that her older sister was bugging her so she gave her a one-two punch in the head! This usually very calm, reasonable child had gotten a bit tired of her older sister's antics and thought this would solve the problem.

My husband and I went on to explain to them that this was the training ground for them to learn to get along so that someday when they were married, they would get along with their husbands. The one-two punch would surely not be a good conflict resolution measure for their future marriages! We recognized that we definitely needed to continue working in this area with these two.

You see, it is in the everyday, day-in-day-out practice that we will make a difference in the choices our kids make outside our homes. We don't want to raise a generation of weaklings who cannot stand up to the pressures of culture as soon as they leave the shelter of the family home. Every time we encourage them to take the opportunity to deny themselves, resolve a conflict with their siblings, or stand for what is right, we are helping them develop their purity muscles.

# Chapter 8

# TALKING ABOUT THE
# BIRDS AND THE BEES

Now if there's anything that makes most
parents nervous, it's talking to their kids
about sex. From time to time I come
across someone in the medical profession who can
articulate for their children all about the birds
and the bees without butterflies in their stomach,
but that is not the case for most of us. So let's get
started!

## The First Message

I believe we want to begin talking age-appropriately
with our children when they are three or four years
old. It will come up at age two with some kids, the

ones who are constantly asking questions and want to know all the facts. Now I know this is young, but I would much rather give my kids a godly message about where babies come from in the context of marriage than to try to undo Hollywood's message about sex. Remember: the first message is the most powerful. It is best to start from scratch with our kids than to have to undo later what they have already heard.

The first place to start when our kids are very young is in talking about the differences between boys and girls. This might seem basic, but when families name body parts, they come up with the most creative designations for the parts below the waist and between the legs. When your kids are babies and you are changing their diapers, practice saying the correct terms. It might take a while to actually say, "p-e-n-i-s," but it will be worth it in the end. Just fast-forward to when your kids are older and you are telling them about how the sperm and the egg meet. This way you will not have to say, "The doodah goes into the wehee," or something to that effect. It is important to use the correct terms from the beginning.

So when you are naming the child's body parts—eyes, hair, arms, and legs—just treat as normal the parts that are covered by a swimsuit too. Also, when your kids are little, you might bathe them together. When they start to notice anatomical differences, it is time to divide and conquer! This is a way of teaching them discretion. When you do this, they learn that privacy and modesty are important.

Your privacy should be important as well. When kids begin to take notice of your private parts, it is time to use discretion. Don't panic, but when it comes to taking showers and changing clothes, just try to have some privacy. If your child runs in to hand you the phone, it is not the end of the world; just quickly grab a towel. I would assume this to be obvious, but I have met a handful of parents of young children who told me that they do not wear any clothing at home around the house. Yes, you just read that correctly; they walk around naked. This might not be the best approach to reinforce purity in your home!

A question that I am asked frequently is whether or not to wait until kids ask a question about how babies are made to share with them about the facts of life. I do believe that some children question everything, and this timing may work for those children. Sometimes this question comes up earlier than many of us would believe. With that said, others of us have kids who will never bring up subjects like this, even when they are twenty-five! Always plan to talk to your kids on at least an annual basis about this subject.

Many parents of very young children fear that

after they have lovingly shared with them all these delicate matters, their children will go to Sunday school, raise their hand for show-and-tell, and proceed to expound on everything we said in confidence. This is why when we sit down to share these facts with our youngsters, we want to explain to them that this is a subject that we talk with *only* Mom and Dad about. This way you secure yourself as the source of information—and correct information at that. When your kids know that Mom and Dad love them and are the source for correct information, they will not need to depend on friends or other sources (such as Google). Explain to them that talking with siblings or friends about this subject is off-limits.

Since I get nervous about sharing these details with my children, I have found that having a book in hand makes it easier for me. You can find many great resources that share from a Christian perspective. My favorite for young kids is a book called *The Wonderful Way Babies are Made* by Larry Christenson.[1] It has been around for more than thirty years, and it has a strong Christian perspective, beginning with Creation. It also has a wonderful section on adoption, which is a subject that most books like this do not cover.

I have a variety of books on hand, and in the spring of each year I sit down with each of my young children and read one together with them. I don't do it with lots of fanfare; I just read it to them as I would any other story that we enjoy together. Having books on hand is part of my intentional plan to help them grow in their understanding year by year beginning when they are three. I simply want to help them understand God's design for sex within marriage and how babies are made.

With each passing year, I get a different reaction. It is not enough to do this one time and hope they will remember it. Think of how many different messages are being directed toward our kids about sex—hundreds, if not thousands. Just standing in the checkout line at the grocery store is bad enough if your child can read! We need to maintain an unyielding message in the face of the onslaught coming toward our children.

Another area we want to cover with our kids who are elementary age and younger is appropriate touch. It seems that everyone I know these days has personally had an experience, or knows someone well who has had an experience, with being sexually molested. This is horribly tragic and much more common than we realize. This is not the same world we grew up in, and we need to take precautions and protect our children. It is simple to even teach little ones that no one except those you have clearly specified may touch them in the areas that their swimsuit covers. *The Swimsuit Lesson* by Jon Holsten does a fantastic job of explaining this sensitive subject to children. In the story he writes, "If anyone ever touches you, or even tries to touch you on your private parts—you must tell Mom or Dad. Even if the person tells you not to say anything."[2] This is the first step in protecting your children from sexual abuse; they must feel comfortable in telling you about anyone or anything that has crossed that boundary. Research also shows that children who know the proper names for their body parts are less likely to be sexually abused.[3]

Additional caution concerns the fact that such abuse does not involve only predatory adults. This hit home one day when I was talking to an acquaintance who is a family physician. After I mentioned problems that boys struggling with pornography have, she shared an experience with me. She told me that in the same week she had seen two patients, both little girls, who had been molested. One was five years old and one was eight. The most shocking part of the story was that they had both been molested by fourteen-year-old boys! This is becoming much more common as boys are becoming addicted to pornography at a younger age and as they become more and more entrenched in perversion. What they are watching leads them to act out on innocent victims.

To keep your children safe, you need to be alert. Do you know what the older sibling of that neighbor friend your child is playing with every afternoon is doing on the computer? Keep tabs on the kids playing at your home. Don't just assume they are fine if they are playing upstairs or in the basement (or anywhere you can't see them). As parents it's often tempting to let our kids go off and play together while we do chores or catch up with their parents on the latest happenings. But we should never neglect to check in with our kids and find out what they are playing.

Once while staying with some friends, I went to check in with our kids. My friend's ten-year-old daughter looked up at me as I walked in and immediately got quiet. She shot my daughter a look that spoke volumes. I immediately created an activity that they could do while within eyesight (and earshot) of her mom and me. Later when I questioned my daughter about what they had been talking about, she shared that her friend had just started to talk about sex. Because I had always instructed her to only speak with her father and me about sex, she was trying to figure out how to excuse herself from the conversation when I walked in. I'm so glad I walked in when I did!

## THE MOVE TOWARD MATURITY

As our kids move into their tween years, puberty is just around the corner. We will start with girls because they reach this time of growth first. This provides such a wonderful opportunity to talk to our daughters about growing up.

When my oldest daughter was nine years old, I was getting my hair cut one day. The gal cutting my hair had a daughter a year older than my daughter. As we chatted, she mentioned that she had heard that girls are maturing physically more quickly these days and that our daughters would probably get their periods two years earlier than we did when we were preteens. I was so shocked that I quickly jerked my head to look with horror in her direction—just at the moment her scissors snipped. (That's when my entire hairstyle changed for a season because she cut a huge chunk out of the back of my hair!)

I had thought I had a couple more years before I needed to share with my daughter about that part of growing up. This was a reality check, and it woke me up to the fact that I had better begin sooner rather than later. I began the search for a book. (Remember, I like to have a book in hand when I share about all these types of details.) I could not find one anywhere. The most popular choice of most moms I knew was not even a Christian resource; it introduced the topic of boyfriends and so forth, which were areas that I did not want to get into at this point in my daughter's life.

I wanted to speak to her about this one subject from a godly perspective. I didn't want to talk with her about everything from her physical development to a boy's physical development to boyfriends to sex all in one sitting! So I ended up getting together with some moms and daughters and wrote a series called Beautifully Made. This three-book set is appropriate from the age of eight on up because of the fact that some girls mature early. I would advise talking to your daughter by age nine or at the latest ten, even if she is not developing yet, lest she hear about menstruation from someone besides you. The first book of Beautifully Made, called *Approaching Womanhood*, is a simple way to share with your daughter about her developing body in a way that celebrates how God is growing her into a unique young woman.

I always try to focus on being positive with my daughters when talking to them about menstruation. I never refer to it as being a "curse." In fact, I try to celebrate with my girls when their periods start. I have found it to be a good idea to get prepared ahead of time by filling a gift bag with a selection of pads and items they will need when they start their first period. I include the second book in the Beautifully Made series (this book, *Celebrating Womanhood*, is designed to give to them when they start their period with practical advice and answers to common questions every girl wants to know) and some fun little gift items that I know that particular girl would enjoy. Then

I place the bag in the very top of my closet and wait for the day when she comes to tell me that her period has started. When that moment arrives, I know I have a gift I can pull out and give to her to start her celebration of moving into womanhood. This arrangement has always worked very well, except the time one of my daughters started when we were on vacation. Oh, well, for the best-laid plans…out the door we went to Walmart. We also might share a special meal or get her hair cut, and Dad always brings her a bouquet of flowers. He knows his daughters are always embarrassed by the fact that Mom "told" Dad, but they also feel very loved.

Now I know about one girl whose mom called all the relatives and threw a party for her daughter when she had her first period. I talked to the daughter some time afterward, and she was still embarrassed! While celebrating, it's important to value your daughter's privacy, as this is so new and personal to them.

## BOYS' DEVELOPMENT

A lady once shared with me that she always reminds her fifteen-year-old son about purity by saying something like this: "Son, my job is to deliver you pure to your wife on your wedding day." Wow, there's a mom with clear expectations for her son!

Although boys' development occurs later than girls, be sure you explain all the details yourself, before his "well-meaning" friends get the opportunity. That means you need to begin when your son is young. In my work with preteens, I have found that boys make more significant decisions about their purity and future decisions when they are eleven years old than at any other age. Now I know, Mom, he is still your little boy (with emphasis on "little"). But this seems to be a key age for setting convictions and values. Dennis Rainey of *FamilyLife Today* talks about how eleven and twelve is the age when our boys and girls are setting their convictions and values for the future.[4] Don't miss this window of opportunity by thinking your son is too innocent for these topics. It is far easier to talk to our kids before they "like" someone than to wait until it is an issue. I have had so many moms say to me one year at a conference that their son is too young, only to confide at the next year's conference that they wish they had taken the now-missed opportunity.

I have found the book *Lintball Leo's Not-So-Stupid Questions About Your Body* by Dr. Walt Larimore to be an engaging resource for teaching your son about his development. Whether you read it together or he reads it by himself, make sure you read it too. Being able to engage your son in conversations about physical development, even if the discussions feel a bit uncomfortable, is a key component of informing your son. Larimore writes: "Puberty can be a pretty confusing time....But it helps if you remember it's all a part of growing up. God made your body and this is the way He wants it to work—so don't sweat it."[5]

Now the taboo topic that parents ask me about all the time. Masturbation. Yes, I said the word, and to keep everyone calm I will call it the "m" word from now on. I have found when it comes to this subject (and believe me, I don't pretend to be an expert), there are two opposing viewpoints: (1) Do it all you want. (2) Don't do it at all, or it will fall off.

While I know these are two extremes, let me give you my two cents. The traditional psychological advice is, "Don't make any big deal out of this." I believe that this is no longer the best guidance, largely because there is so much more availability of pornography today than even a few years ago. When we parents turn a blind eye to the temptation facing our young men, we may only launch them into a lifelong struggle. Taking the other extreme of imposing utmost guilt does not help the situation either, because it causes our boys to fall into condemnation and feel they can never escape the lure of the "m" word.

The best advice is not to ignore it, but not to encourage it. We need to teach our sons not to entertain lustful thoughts. (See Matthew 5:28, Romans 8:5; 13:14; and James 1:14–15 for some clear biblical imperatives.) It is important to talk about purity of mind and heart with our boys, because we want to equip them to win the battle with lust and not leave any foothold for the enemy. We need to help them keep track of what is going on in their heads. Some friends have a fifteen-year-old son who struggles with this issue. Whenever he is tempted, he will immediately call his dad to help distract him. His dad will then talk with him in an encouraging manner, encouraging him to go play some basketball or to find another distraction for that very moment. This is a good example of parents playing as a team to help their sons fight the battle that tries at every moment to take them down.

Of course this approach takes time, but it will always be time well invested. This is not a boys-only issue, but it is something that affects our daughters as well (58 percent of seventeen-year-old girls have done it!).[6]

This also takes parents who are willing to look at the real issues with their kids. It can be tough to ask yourself: *Do I really want to know what is going on?* The reason you want to know is one study shows "masturbation in adolescence appears to be tied to other types of behavior, including…a greater likelihood of engaging in sexual relations with a partner."[7] If your answer is yes, then I encourage you to seek to know what is going on behind your kids' closed doors, so that you can become their true ally in the fight for purity of heart, mind, and body.

## THE TALK

Although you may have had many conversations with your preteens about how babies are made, I do believe it is good to have "the talk" at some point. There is no magic age, but around eleven or twelve is a good time to get away from home and not only go over the birds and the bees, but also set standards for future relationships.

> It is best to have "the talk" too early, rather than too late.

This provides a wonderful opportunity for a weekend away with just father/son or mother/daughter. In our family we use it as part of a series of rites of passage that we do, and we always take our kids before they turn twelve. It is best to do it too early rather than too late. If your children are enrolled in a school setting where they have sex education classes, make certain that you take them for this special time before they start that class. Remember—this time with them includes more than just going over facts; it's a time for equipping their character to stand strong for the future.

I recommend picking a special place where the

two of you would love to go. Some families find a cabin or go camping. I had one mom tell me that she took her daughter on a cruise! Just do not do "the talk" right at home; go someplace out of the ordinary. Even finding a hotel or a cabin that is only an hour from home can be a good option.

I highly recommend using the resource *Passport2Purity* by Dennis and Barbara Rainey[8] for your weekend away. It is basically your weekend retreat in a box. I have spoken with thousands of parents who have done this with their kids, and I have used it myself. Parents always say something along the lines of, "The *Passport2Purity* weekend was one of the best weekends we ever spent together." Whether you choose to follow a particular resource or you plan "the talk" yourself, be sure you include not only the birds and the bees but also information about setting values and boundaries for the future, as well as clear expectations for dating or courtship relationships.

Well before one parent takes the son or daughter away for this special weekend together, Mom and Dad should set aside a time to discuss boundaries and expectations for the future. This includes setting an age that dating or courtship is appropriate or how it will look for your family. Have a strategy prepared for if your child gets asked out on a date. (This is not just for girls, but boys are often asked out by overly aggressive girls as well.) Both parents should be in agreement about their children's future romance and relationships, as well as their suggested guidelines for physical purity.

There is a lot of ground between holding hands and having sex, and our children need to understand that staying pure is not about technical virginity. It is about setting up an intentional plan to stay pure long before the opportunity ever arrives. Many of those of us who are now parents were told "just don't have sex." No one ever bothered to spell out a strategy for how to make this a reality. If there was ever a time that kids need more than "just don't do it" and a plan for purity, it is in this generation!

This weekend away will make possible a special one-on-one time that will open the lines of communication and build the relationship. That being said, you should expect different reactions from different kids when you share this kind of information. Some kids remain quiet and never say a word or ask a question. Some ask lots of questions. Some express themselves in unexpected ways. In fact, one dad told me that after his son heard how the sperm and egg meet, his son got up and ran off into the forest. (He did come back!) It *is* a bit embarrassing, and you can expect a lot of laughter. Different reactions are natural.

## "The Talk" and Your Own Past

I have spoken with so many different parents who hesitate to have "the talk" with their children because they made poor choices while they were growing up. Almost every one of these people is terrified that their son or daughter will look up at them while they are talking about boundaries and say, "Well, Mom [or Dad], what did *you* do?"

I have a bit of guidance that I give to parents at this moment. Since you are sharing with a child who is eleven or twelve years old, they are still relatively young. This is not the time to share "all" unless the Holy Spirit moves you to do so. You could respond in a couple different ways.

The first way is to think of something you did *right* and be ready to share it at that point. Surely in all your mistakes you can find one thing that you did correctly and share it with your child. The other way you could approach it is by acknowledging something like, "The generation that I grew up in made serious mistakes when it came to dating, and I am so sorry that you have inherited the consequences in your generation today."

What's most important for our kids is to understand the reasons to stay pure. When they get older, with the Lord's leading and in God's timing, you can share the struggles and victories you have faced on your own journey. Don't let the enemy make you afraid to share with your child if you have struggled in the past or you currently struggle with any kind of sexual sin. Jesus died on the cross to set every generation free from the bondage of sin. Instead, as you look at your own child's generation, let that give you a renewed reason to cling to Jesus, bring your sin to the cross, and start fresh. Do everything that you can to get free. God wants to use you to break the bondage so your children can be free, but it needs to start today with you, or your children will follow in your footsteps.

# Chapter 9

# NOT AWAKENING ROMANCE

Now that the birds and bees talk is out of the way, let's talk about what is really luring our kids to become sexually impure: Hollywood's ideas about romance and relationships. As the big screen imposes its love agenda, this larger-than-life viewpoint draws most unsuspecting kids right into its grip and drags them out to sea with the rushing tide of our culture.

After working with thousands of teens, we have found that the top lies about relationships are soaked in media exposure. They fall along these lines:

🔒 I'm worthless unless someone is attracted to me.

- I have to be in a relationship to be accepted by my peers.

- *Everyone* else is doing it!

- I am defined by what other people think of me.

- I am not complete unless I am in a romantic relationship.

- Casual romantic relationships won't hurt me.

Underlying the enemy's list of lies is the one that says God is not enough for me, and I am not complete unless I have someone or something else. That ever-deep hunger in each of us that can be filled only by the living God causes us to go searching. The enemy takes advantage of this to persuade people, especially kids, that if only they had that amazing romantic relationship, everything in them would be satisfied. People who dive into a lifestyle of relationship after relationship to quench that desire find that this is the farthest thing from the truth.

Here again we need to begin working with our kids while they are still young, giving them a picture of the love story that God has in store for them. Every single person has a sacred love story that begins with Him. None of us will find full satisfaction anywhere else. A verse in the Song of Solomon directs us not to fall for all the romance that is offered to us from all sides. Here is Song of Solomon 2:7 in three different translations:

> Don't excite love, don't stir it up, until the time is ripe—and you're ready.
>
> —THE MESSAGE

> Do not stir up or awaken love until the appropriate time.
>
> —HCSB

> Promise me...not to awaken love until the time is right.
>
> —NLT

## YOUNG "LOVE"

When I look around me, I see four primary influences that open our kids' hearts to premature romance:

- Screen media
- Books
- Music
- Friends

Romance fills the screen in movies and TV. Hollywood portrays its own picture of how life should fall into place and how love should unfold.

When you notice your son or daughter walking away from the latest movie saying, "I wish I had a love story like that!", you know that the movie they just saw has awakened romantic love. It has opened the door of their hearts to desire the world's brand of romance. Your kids do not have to be teenagers for this to happen. It could be your four-year-old daughter who has stars in her eyes after watching the latest and greatest Disney princess movie. This is a dynamic principle we should watch for in our kids no matter what their age.

Books also unlock the door to romance. Now our young gentlemen are off the hook for this one because I rarely see guys reading romance novels. But our girls—this one is for them. I'm not talking only about secular romance, which you can find everywhere, but also the Christian romance novels that are out there. We all know how great it is to sit down with a heroic novel that whisks us away to another place in time, but so many of these books result in a desire for forbidden romance. When our daughters read romantic stories, their hearts are opened to seeds of romance that, when planted, will germinate into something they are not yet ready for.

Another big opening to romance in our young people comes through music. In this area I definitely see as many young men fall prey as young women. Love songs bring out the heroic desires in all guys. They are drawn to the knight who pursues the love of the young maiden and to the romantic singer who strums a serenade on the guitar to his secret love. Music truly opens the heart to romance in such a powerful way that we see new genres of love songs in every generation, and their influence extends for decades.

In addition to screen media, books, and music, friends are very influential in awakening notions of romantic love in our kids. If your children are surrounded by close friends who are all charging full speed ahead, pursuing the illusion of romance, this will surely have an impact on your child. It becomes difficult for them not to become enmeshed in this way of thinking. Take note if every conversation contains references to whomever "he likes" and "she likes."

When our kids have indulged in these romantic pastimes, they can easily spend hours being the movie director of a romance that is debuting in their minds. They can write a detailed script in which they are the leading stars, and they rehearse scenes over and over in their minds. Lies from this fantasy get planted and begin to grow. Sometimes, action scenes that were produced in their minds and hearts can lead to tangible action in their daily lives.

Where are your kids living? In a fantasy world

they have created in their minds or in the reality in which God has placed them? This is distinctly different from the invisible world of a five-year-old, filled with new friends and interesting activities. I'm talking about the fantasy world of your daughter who is fifteen, daydreaming endlessly about that guy she saw on the big screen at the movies or that boy she saw at the mall last weekend. God calls our kids to grow up and to grow into reality.

We have to realize that this worldly romantic love meets a hunger in our fallen nature. It's like chocolate. I love dark chocolate. Yet if I had never tasted dark chocolate, I would never have developed an appetite for it. There are some days when I crave that wonderful bite of dark chocolate! I hunger for it. The same is true when our children awaken romantic love. They develop an appetite and a hunger for it. Their demand needs to be satisfied. They yearn for more and more to meet the increasing demand.

## HUNGER FOR GOD

Do your teens feast on the world's menu, or are they developing a hunger for the living God? Have they tasted and seen that the Lord is good? Our kids need our help in this area. By discipling them, we can help them learn to hunger for the Lord and to give up the insatiable appetites of this

world. We want them to be able to echo the words
of the psalm:

> Teach me your way, O Lord, and I will
> walk in your truth; give me an undivided
> heart, that I may fear your name.
>
> —Psalm 86:11, niv

Now I was one of those kids who was impacted
by all of the factors I have listed above. When I was
around ten or eleven years old, I began to be swept
away by TV programs and movies about love and
relationships. I launched into reading books solely
focused on romance. Love songs filled my heart
with starry-eyed dreams. By thirteen I was certain
that I would someday serenade my true love while
basking in the rays of a beautiful sunset on a for-
saken stretch of beach. My friends all the while
spurred me on with one guy after another to "like."

During this season of my life I also came to
know the Lord in a very real way. I had a true
desire in my heart to follow after God. I spent
time in His Word and was active in my youth
group. The problem was that my heart was divided.

You see, I wanted to follow the Lord with my
whole heart, but pursuing the world's ideas of
romance divided my heart, preventing me from
following after the Lord 100 percent. God does
not want us to pay attention only to not awakening
love, but the imperative key factor is that He wants

us *to awaken love for Him.* Our love life needs to begin with falling deeply in love with the Lord. We can tell our kids not to awaken their hearts to romantic love, but if they do not understand that the most important factor is really awakening love in their hearts for the Lord Jesus Christ and God Almighty, they will be lost.

The foundation of our personal life must be our depth of love for the Lord. Every other relationship grows out of this foundation—or the lack of it. If our love for the Lord is deeply rooted, then secure love for others sprouts from this. Every relationship flows from this foundation. I am convinced that this is why the enemy spends so much time and effort polluting our ideas about love. He knows that if he can corrupt our foundational love, then our lives will be built on the sand and not the rock of Jesus Christ.

*If our love for the Lord is deeply rooted, then secure love for others sprouts from this.*

Especially while your kids are young, this is the time for their spiritual life to take root. Like no other time this is the season in their lives to awaken love for the Lord. It is the foundation-building season. But how can we combat all the factors that propel them to awaken romantic love? When we see that romantic love has been awakened, we can take some practical steps to put it back to sleep.

## PUTTING ROMANTIC LOVE BACK TO SLEEP

For example, if you notice that the latest Hollywood blockbuster has unlocked the door of romance in your child's life, then it's time to do some fasting. Now I'm not talking about not eating popcorn and candy, but fasting from certain kinds of screen media. It's part of putting romantic love back to sleep. This doesn't mean we have to cut the cable TV and never see another movie, but purposeful fasting from movies and TV with any romantic content may be in order.

A young lady that I mentored has a great testimony of how God moved on her heart to fall more deeply in love with Him when she was nineteen years old. Sure, she was "old enough" to pursue romantic relationships, but God challenged her to build a strong foundation by making Jesus Christ her first love. Everyone else around her was diving into significant relationships at about this same time. God asked her to dive into a deep relationship with Him and to make Him her first love.

To rise to His challenge, she knew that she would have to start fasting from romantic books and movies. She committed herself to focus on falling deeply in love with Jesus for the next year. She gave up all of the romance movies and went to the action ones instead. With all the romance novels pushed aside, God challenged her to dig deeply into His Word.

After that year was complete, love in her heart was so awakened to God that going to see the latest "chick flick" didn't have the same pull on her heart anymore. In fact, her need for romance had been met by the living God.

You might consider encouraging your kids to fast from things that awaken romance in their hearts. Guys would need to limit their exposure to the visual stimulation that breeds lust in their minds, while girls would need to say no to the tainted love stories that Hollywood plants in their minds (i.e., the promise of the handsome hunk who meets a girl's every emotional need and rescues her out of a difficult situation).

Steer your kids clear of romance novels, and help them keep from getting hooked on them. Encourage them to try a different genre. They can find a multitude of books out there that are full of the adventures of heroes of the Christian faith; such books would help them in their walk with the Lord.

Find ways to help your kids deepen their love relationship with their heavenly Father. Tell them how every person has an innate deep desire for intimacy, and how romance novels or romantic music and movies stir up that longing inside each of us. Explain to them that we cannot expect to enjoy deep intimacy with our spouses until we have satisfied that deep-down longing for spiritual intimacy. Our love story with the Lord comes first.

Music, after all, was first designed for worshiping the Lord God in heaven. Since the fall of Lucifer (who was the first "worship leader" before God's throne) it has been perverted and reduced to a mere imitation of its original purpose.

Falling more deeply in love with Jesus is the goal, and worship is a key. With true worship music, whether in a corporate context or just listening alone, you can bring the redemptive focus of music back to your kids, and you can help them fall more deeply in love with Jesus. A life of worship will help to put a heart awakened to romance back to sleep and awaken love for the Lord instead.

Encourage your kids to find worship music that they enjoy. Start worshiping as a family as well. This was a first step for our kids in learning to love worship. It's not as if my husband and I play the guitar or piano and have amazing musical talent to make this work. No, we just love to worship the Lord. It may not sound like the latest recording artist, but that's OK. We started one year during the Christmas season. During our family devotions we would pick out a Christmas carol or two to sing together. It became a time of worship, and our whole family began to look forward to it. Then we began to share our favorite worship songs. The seeds that were sown during these family times, although they might not have sounded like the local church worship team, grew into a deeper love for God all around.

We can also encourage our teens to write their own worship songs and music. They have an incredible amount of creativity. Some of us are parents to creative artists who thrive when they can compose, paint, or script their love for the Lord.

## Developing a Love Story With God

Because of the fact that our kids can experience tremendous pressure from their peers to follow what everyone else is doing in terms of romance and relationships, we need to do everything we can to help our kids develop their own love story with God. We need to encourage them to grasp onto God's everlasting truth and show them that it is worth standing against what our culture holds so dear.

It is difficult for them when they are conscious of being in the minority among their friends. This is the point where you can motivate them to find at least one friend who embraces the same standard they do, and they can stick together. The challenge is that sometimes that friend does not appear right away. When my kids feel that they don't have the friendships that they desire, I remind them that their best friend is always waiting for them: God is a friend who sticks closer than a brother. (See Proverbs 18:24.)

In this season in our kids' lives when we have the opportunity to give them a vision of a love story with the Lord, we have to spend time cultivating this love story. We also have to counter the lies of the enemy as the world tries to supplant our first love, Jesus Christ.

I want to conclude this chapter with a testimony from Katherine, a beautiful young lady in her twenties who is on my staff. She is an example of a young person who has found her first love.

---

A while back I was going through a particularly hard time. I was super-bugged that I was the only one who wasn't on the road to marriage. We were in Indonesia, and I have no idea why this whole marriage thing was so hard then, but it was. I found myself totally doubting God and questioning His goodness. I would sit in on Julie's talks to teens and hear her tell them, "God has written a love story for each one of you." And then I would sit there and think, "Yeah…everyone but me." This thought led me to wonder, "What if it's God's will for me to be single the rest of my life?" So then my thought progression went to: "So am I the only one He *hasn't* written a love story for?" These thoughts made me doubt God's goodness.

Because I know that being a hypocrite on a ministry trip is really not a good idea, I got up early one morning, Bible and devo in hand. I sat in an old chair, hearing the Muslim morning call to prayer, and I was just broken before God. I was really honest—"God, I'm not moving until I get something from You. I can't keep up the façade of being content when I'm not." I felt led to open the book I was reading, *Hinds Feet on High Places* by Hannah Hurnard. I was already quite a way into the book, but for some reason began to read Hannah's preface to the allegory, which I had previously skipped. Toward the end she explains that God created marriage and singleness for the same purpose. Both equally teach us about the love that God has for us. They do it really differently, but one isn't better than the other. After reading that, I asked God to show me what He was trying tell me. And at that moment I experienced one of those times when you feel God speak to you, if you know what I mean. It's hard to describe. It went like this:

*Me: God, have You written a love story for me? What if I never get married? Am I just missing out?*

*God: Katherine...I have written a love story for you. And that love story is with Me. If I have you get married, that will just be an extension of our love story. But it started with Me, and it's going to end with Me.*

At that point I just started to cry.

Being single, despite what (literally) most of the world says, is not inferior to being married. It's an opportunity for us to develop a love story with God.

# Chapter 10

# THE DATING GAME

WHILE OUR KIDS are very young, even in preschool, we can begin to set the paradigm for what our families will do when it comes to the dating game.

Dating comes off like an Olympic event in some families. They commence training when their sons and daughters are young, so they can win some medal by the time they arrive in high school. In other families parents have fond memories of their dating years, and they want their children to reap the rewards of an environment similar to the one they grew up in.

But neither approach will work in this day and age. Our kids face a minefield of hidden snares and obstacles that they must be prepared for if they are going to enter the dating game. If they decide to play this game, it entails much more than traditional dating customs. The new playing field includes friends with benefits, sexting, hooking up, and cyber sex. This means taking the time while they are little to invest in deciding what direction your family will take.

> *My husband and I set out to shape the kids' future view of love and romance so that it would be in line with the Word of God.*

I began to realize this would be an issue for our family when we kept having girls. My husband was certain it would be sufficient to start collecting hunting rifles, so he could meet our daughters' potential dates while cleaning these weapons on the front porch! I figured at that point the boys would not drop by at all, and we had better come up with another plan.

## SETTING THE STRATEGY

As I have been describing in previous chapters, my husband and I set out to shape the kids' future view of love and romance so that it would be in line with the Word of God and not the world. One of the first things we did was to begin praying for their future spouses on a regular basis. We always try to pray together before we fall asleep, and this became a regular petition. We let our kids know what we were praying for, and we told them that we are believing God to bring them a spouse whose heart is sold out for the Lord and His kingdom.

And then we start working on an approach to sexual purity. There are so many pressures in our world today to compromise purity, even for very young children. Even if we parents can't imagine how purity could be an issue for five- or six-year-olds, I always remember one of my favorite children's stories, *The Princess and the Kiss* by Jennie Bishop.[1] It is about a king and queen who are entrusted with their daughter's first kiss on the day she is born. When the daughter comes of age, they explain that she may give away her first kiss to whomever she chooses, but to remember a first kiss is given just one time. The princess is wise because she has many suitors come to offer her anything she could ask for in exchange for her first kiss, but she waits and waits. Finally a young man comes along who cherishes the princess and her first kiss—in fact, he has also saved his first kiss just for her. They share their first kiss on their wedding day. This is a wonderful story to share with both our sons and daughters to encourage them to save their first kiss for their wedding day. (Even though it is about a princess, we need to share it with our sons too, or we will just have a generation of girls saving their first kiss!)

Jennie Bishop, who wrote this enchanting story,

shared with me how the idea for this book came about. When her oldest daughter was five and in kindergarten, she came home one day, and the conversation went something like this:

"Mom, everyone has a boyfriend. My one friend got a boyfriend today. My other friend dumped her boyfriend today. My other friend kissed her boyfriend today. And I want one too!"

Her mother, who was shocked and surprised to hear that this was going on in kindergarten, got on her knees that night and began seeking the Lord. He then gave her the idea for this story.

Now I know that this idea is a leap for some of us. The first time I ever heard of someone saving his or her first kiss for her wedding day was from family friends whose daughter had met a young man. She had never kissed anyone. (She is a beautiful and talented young woman, but God had arranged to protect her, and the opportunity never came up.) When she was in her early twenties, she met a young man, and her heart was all aflutter because she felt that he was "the one." In their first few weeks of seeing each other he sat down with her and expressed that he would like to marry her someday and that he wanted to wait to save their first kiss for their wedding day! She was stunned. She didn't know whether to be excited or a bit disappointed. She had never heard of this happening in real life. But when her wedding day finally did arrive, the presence of God was unmatched because the two of them possessed such purity of spirit.

Now I am hearing this same story more and more frequently from couples all over the world. Young people who are committed to purity are taking this extreme stand because they want to avoid the many stumbling blocks along the road of physical relationships. They realize that no matter how pure couples try to be when they start out, it is difficult to put on the brakes once they are on the road of physical involvement. God is raising up young people all over the world who know that having an extremely high standard is vital for the age we live in.

Now is this approach for everyone? The decision must be led by the Spirit of God; a young person needs to prayerfully consider where his or her boundaries should be. For my part I am strongly encouraging my daughters to save their first kiss for their wedding day. I started with reading them stories such as *The Princess and the Kiss* when they were two or three years old. This does not seem to be too young, especially in the face of evidence from parents who share that their five- or six-year-olds have already given away their first kiss! Now I know that this is just playground politics affecting kids' behavior—the "she likes so and so" and "he likes so and so" banter—but if the pressure is this strong while they are still in kindergarten, what will it be like when they reach middle school? At that point they will be giving away much more than their first kiss! Why not motivate our children to save their first kiss as long as possible? That is why I am always encouraging my kids to do this. I know that at some point saving the first kiss for marriage will have to be their own commitment and not just Mom and Dad's good idea.

I also think of the practical side of this standard. How much better it is to rally behind them to save their first kiss instead of simply saying, "Don't have sex." Then if they choose to kiss after all, the consequences of going below that standard are not nearly as dire as if they choose to go below the do-not-have-sex standard.

As you well know, the consequences of having sex before marriage go well beyond the traditional fears of getting pregnant or contracting an STD (although those are very real concerns too!). Check out some of the findings reported by Physiciansforlife.org:

- Those who are sexually active before marriage have greater behavioral problems.

- Those who live together before marriage suffer from greater depression and anxiety.

✛ Those who are sexually active before marriage are much more likely to divorce.

✛ Those who have had premarital sex are more likely to have extramarital affairs.[2]

Now I know some of you who are reading this think it's crazy, because you have never met a young person who is committed to saving that first kiss. Well, I know dozens of young people who are committed to doing it. I have a team of young people who are in their twenties and who are walking this out. An engaged couple on my team commented to me that when you don't kiss, you spend a lot more time talking; you actually to get to know each other when you aren't distracted by the physical.

Some people have expressed another concern in this area: "If we don't kiss before we're married, how will we know if we are physically compatible? What if it turns out that I don't even like kissing this person?" My response to that is simply this: You cannot express such a concern if you are truly in love. If you grow to love someone for who that person is on the inside, for the incredible person that God has created him or her to be, to the level that you plan to get married—don't worry; the physical satisfaction is going to come! It is part of the intimacy of marriage, not a "test drive" that you take with your boyfriend or girlfriend before your wedding day.

## THE DATING YEARS

It seems to me that when I was a girl, many families had a general rule that their kids could start dating at sixteen. I am not really sure who came up with this magical age, but if you have a sixteen-year-old at your house, you know that in the majority of cases the emotional maturity level at this age is not relationship-worthy. Now, your sixteen-year-old may disagree with me. (We believe we can accomplish anything when we are that age, right?)

The fact is that when kids start the cycle of being in and out of relationships much younger than sixteen, when the relationship cycle gets underway at a younger and younger age, the consequences of the physical relationships ramp up. Consider this: 91 percent of girls who start dating at age twelve have sex before they are out of high school.[3] When we allow our boys or girls to be in seemingly "innocent" relationships at a young age, we're actually setting them up for failure.

We also should look at the relative stage of brain development at this time of a child's life. The fact is that our kids' brains are not fully developed until they are twenty-five. The book *Hooked: New Science on How Casual Sex Is Affecting Our*

*Children*[4] is a phenomenal resource for explaining how the development of the human brain and body chemistry affect teenage sexual experimentation. We parents should take into consideration the fact that the cycle of being in and out of physical relationships so young creates in children's brain chemistry the need for a greater depth of physical affection every time they delve into a new relationship.

We need to understand that, in fact, the chemicals released in the brain actually glue us together when there is physical interaction between the sexes. Now when you think about this in terms of marriage, this is part of the wonder of God's amazing design. When we have a physical component to our marriages, we find that we are stuck together so that no one can separate us. We all need that, right?

The problem arises when there is a physical component in a relationship outside of marriage. When the glue that sticks people together gets ripped apart constantly and then stuck together again in relationship after relationship, the "stickiness" begins to wane. Then when we finally find ourselves in a marriage, it's as if the "glue" comes into the marriage damaged and malfunctioning.

When I first read the research, I was shocked about the extent of physical touch required to put these principles into action. It takes as little as a twenty-second hug! Kids can be chemically glued to each other through a brief, twenty-second contact? In working with youth, how often do I see young people not only hugging but also sitting on each other's laps, giving massages, and generally hanging all over each other? We need to communicate to our children the impact of their actions!

Keeping the future in view is an important element, because kids can't do it without help. When I was a teenager, I thought mostly about myself and about that day's activities. I had no concept of how my actions might have negative consequences in the future. This phenomenon occurs because the area of our brains that is responsible for long-term planning (the prefrontal cortex) is not yet fully developed during the teen years. This is why teens will take risks that an adult usually will not. The reliable perspective from Mom and Dad during this season needs to be an anchor for their children.

## VISION FOR THE FUTURE

As a result of all that I've read and observed, I am encouraging my kids not to date during their teen years. And when opportunity presents itself to them, which it does on a regular basis in our culture today, I take the time and energy to steer them to God's vision for their future. This takes hard work and lots of late-night talking, as we set clear boundaries and expectations (and sometimes consequences). I want to keep my children from awakening romantic love. I use different tactics depending on the circumstances. Sometimes fasting from certain media or technology has become the answer. The essential thing is to walk closely, side-by-side with my teens, confronting issues as they come up with the Holy Spirit's leading.

## ALL THE DAYS OF YOUR LIFE

After reading a book by a friend of mine, I was encouraged to look at a verse in Proverbs 31 in a different light.[5] Verse 12 states, "She brings him good, not harm, all the days of her life" (NLT). I had read this verse many times before, but suddenly it jumped out at me that it says, "*all* the days of her life." It doesn't mean I honor my husband from the day I get married on, but *every* day of my life! How am I instructing my daughters to bring honor to their future husbands even before they meet them? (Guys, I'm afraid you're on the hook for this one too, because I do not believe that God is partial or has a double standard.) This means that instead of flowing with our culture and stepping into the revolving door of one relationship after another, we want to be teaching our kids to honor their future spouses from their earliest days. Now what could that really look like?

First, I think, we could teach them to live as though their future spouses are watching them. Would your son be looking at that girl as if his eyeballs are going to fall out of his head if his wife were sitting right next to him? I hope not! Would your daughter be flirting with that other guy if her future husband were sitting at the table with her? Better not be!

When I am speaking to teens, their pastor is often in the room with us. Usually the pastor is married, and often my husband is with me, so it really makes an impact. I say something like, "I saw you all hanging out earlier before the meeting started, and you were giving each other back-rubs. Now what if your future husband or wife happened to be in the room? Would you still do this?" Usually I get a mixed response to this question. Then I walk over near their pastor and say, "Wouldn't it be really weird if I started to give Pastor Mike a back massage right now?" Most of the time they look at me with big eyes, with expressions of extreme horror on their faces. I continue to make the point of how awkward that would be and how completely inappropriate, because I am married and he is married. I mean, what would his wife think? And what would my husband think? I would *never* do that, and neither would their pastor! But the truth is that our kids do such things all the time—and that does not honor their future spouses. This is one way to communicate to them the importance of honoring that person even though they haven't even met him or her yet.

## LOVE LETTERS

In the book *When God Writes Your Love Story*, Eric Ludy shares how he decided to honor his future wife, so he began to write love letters to her.[6] Before he had even met her, he poured his heart out to her in the letters. He gave them to Leslie on their honeymoon. Now what girl would not love that? The point is that Eric spent years being faithful to Leslie before he even met her. He prayed for his future wife and wrote about his commitment to her. We can encourage our kids to do the same thing.

When I speak to teens, I suggest they do the same thing—that they write letters to their future spouses as a way show their commitment. It happens to be especially great for those kids who are the "hopeless romantics"; it gives them an outlet for those feelings.

One day at a conference I was amused to hear what a girl shared with me. She had heard me speak about Eric's letter idea a few years before, and she had taken my advice. She had done the same thing, and now she was getting married in a couple of months. After I congratulated her, she said there was a unique twist to her story. She said that when she first sat down to write a letter to her future spouse, she did not want to put, "Dear _____." But she didn't know what to put in place of his unknown name. So she just wrote "my cowboy" on the letter. Now the extraordinary thing about this story is that she was about to marry a young man who was a professional rodeo rider—a real cowboy! I told her she might have more of a prophetic gift than she realized!

## IT'S NOT ABOUT ME

Lastly, instead of diving into the dating game with all of its self-indulgence, this is a season to teach our young people to truly live sacrificially now, so they can do so later when they are married. As we who are married know, marriage is not all about me. It is about learning to be selfless and a servant. So many young people who get married find that they have just signed up for a crash course in living for someone besides themselves. It makes for a bumpy beginning that can spiral into destructive patterns and lead to failure.

It is time right now to teach our kids that having to sacrifice what they desire in order to honor another is part of a lifelong commitment to marriage whether they are married yet or not.

So as you have read, I am not a big proponent of our world's view of dating and being in and out of the constant cycle of relationships. I believe our children's teen years should be a season for falling deeply in love with the Lord as they build a strong foundation of preparation for the sacred love story that God has for them in the future. As they sacrifice these dating opportunities at this present moment (and for some there will be lots of sacrifice), they will be establishing their God-given call and destiny.

# Chapter 11

# PURSUING A SACRED
# LOVE STORY

W̲E PARENTS HAVE the opportunity to continue to walk shoulder to shoulder with our children as they grow. Maturing children do not always reflect the contentment and dedication to the Lord that we wish they had. Some do, but others are not quite there yet— and those are the ones who make us parents want to pull out our hair! Because they are still missing the mark, we need to invest time and love in them. The prophet Zephaniah wrote, "Then I will purify the lips of the peoples, that all of them may call on the name of the LORD and serve him *shoulder to shoulder*" (Zeph. 3:9, NIV, emphasis added).

When our children were small, we used to scoop them up into our arms and carry them around. If they were disobedient, we could pick them up and place them in "time out." I remember when it struck me, when my kids reached about ten years of age, as they ran up to jump into my arms, that they were too big to carry anymore. And they only continued to grow bigger! So all the more reason to walk "shoulder to shoulder" with them during the teen years. We still have influence and impact in their lives, but it looks different than it did when they were little.

From when our children are young and throughout their teen years is their time of preparation for their sacred love story. A sacred love story begins with being wholly dedicated to Lord God Almighty. Flowing from a heart that is pure, God has the opportunity to birth a love story that is first dedicated to Him. Going deep with God brings contentment. Out of this place of contentment our kids are not determined to keep pursuing relationship after relationship to fulfill an aching need inside. This is a season for their love of the Lord to be increased and strengthened. This is truly their first love story, as I have mentioned earlier, one that creates a strong foundation for the sacred marital love that is to follow.

Now some of us wonder, "What if my children never get married?" And that could be true, since we know that not all people get married. That is why the focus is not solely on marriage. The foundation created by our children's love story with the Lord is a true foundation whether or not they eventually get married. And we must prepare them for marriage, because ultimately most of them will get married—95 percent, by the time they are fifty-five, will have gotten married.[1]

There are a few broad guidelines for establishing a sacred love story. As parents, I know that we would probably feel more comfortable with a specific formula, and I have seen many very precise templates for the development of love and romance. In general I steer very clear of any fixed set of rules because I know that God is incredibly creative when it comes to this area of our lives. Just as you met your wife or husband in a very different way from how I met mine, I believe God's creativity is too broad to contain in a box. God is the amazing architect of relationships, and everyone's story is unique. He knows what each of us needs, and He makes our love stories unfold differently.

## LEARNING TO HEAR HIS VOICE

Each of us needs to tune an ear to the Lord Almighty when it comes to our kids and whom they will marry. As their parents, though, we need to keep in mind that it is our children who are getting married, and they will have to live day in and day out with their choices. Although parents give counsel and wisdom, it is our children who should ultimately choose their spouses.

So we forgo hard and fast rules for guidelines when we talk about developing a sacred love story with our children. And the first guidelines involve learning to hear the still, small voice of God. Now when it comes to teaching our kids to hear God's voice, picking their husband or wife better not be the arena in which they begin their practice! We have an opportunity as parents to teach our children to discern the voice of God for years while they are growing up. This is vital, because as much as we might be involved in each situation of their young lives and be able to direct them, there comes a point where we must let go. When they go off to college or they move away to take a job somewhere, Mom and Dad are not going to be right there whispering in their ear what choices to make. They need to be able hear and discern God's voice so they can make solid choices on their own.

This training takes place in the tween and teen years, which is the best time to teach our kids how to hear the Lord's voice. I try to teach them this life lesson as it surrounds the little details in their lives. I figure if they know how to recognize God's voice in the little decisions that they have to make every day, it will be clear to them when they are older and they need to make life-changing future decisions. Here's how it can work, for example: When my daughter comes home from a long day and still has a sports practice left in her schedule, she might complain to me about how she does not feel like going. Without declaring that she should or shouldn't go, I simply send her upstairs to pray and ask God whether or not she should go. More times than not she will come down the stairs a while later with her uniform on and ready to go. I'll ask her what God spoke to her, and she will just grin and say, "Mom, I feel like God told me I should go today."

Of course, there are days when we might go through this process and she decides that she will not attend practice. For my part, I always have veto power if I feel that she is not headed in the right direction. But for these situations where I don't have a strong feeling either way, this creates a great opportunity to hear the Lord's voice. There are both triumphs and failures in this arena, and it takes practice and work, for sure!

You are training your child to recognize what God's voice sounds like and how the Lord speaks to them. It's like this: If I as the author of this book called you on the phone, you would not know my voice at all. But if your own dad called you on the phone, you would immediately recognize his voice. It is the same with the voice of God.

At first it is harder to recognize until we become more and more familiar with it.

What are we listening for? For all my kids I teach them to first hear God's voice through Scripture. Whether it comes through what they are reading in their daily devotions or through asking God to lead them to a specific passage, I tell them that I believe that it is God's heart to speak to all His children. He wants to let us know His plan for even the smallest details in our lives. He cares whether or not we go to practice! He wants to lead us moment by moment, not monumental decision by monumental decision. If we have tuned our ears to Him in the small situations, then we can be certain of His guidance in the big decisions.

Here's another example of God giving direction for everyday activities. One of my daughters was praying about whether or not she should go with friends to a lake near our house. She prayed to receive direction through a verse of Scripture. The verse the Lord gave her read as follows: "One day Jesus said to his disciples, 'Let's go over to the other side of the lake.' So they got into a boat and set out" (Luke 8:22, NIV). God definitely cares about the small stuff!

> *He wants to lead us moment by moment, not monumental decision by monumental decision.*

## GOD'S TIMING

The light goes on in our kids' minds when they sincerely listen to the Lord and realize that there is one true God and that He is consistent in His messages to us—and that He speaks about both the everyday things and the big things, such as their personal sacred love story. We had this topic come up the other day with one of our daughters. She had started to pursue a relationship, and when I asked what God had been speaking to her, she said that the Scripture verses God had given her were along the lines of "waiting." This confirmed exactly what my husband and I were receiving as well.

Our kids definitely need to hear from God about whom they are going to marry—and when. This is the most important decision they are ever going to make besides coming to Christ. Knowing beyond the shadow of a doubt that this is where God wants you to be gives peace and confidence through the ups and downs we all face in our marriages.

Hudson Taylor, the great missionary to China, is an incredible example of someone who sought God's timing for marriage. In 1854 he went as a missionary to China, and in the more than fifty years of his life there, 125,000 Chinese people came to Christ. He also established the China Inland

Mission, which sent 849 missionaries to China during his lifetime. What I find interesting about Hudson Taylor is that as a young man, before he left for China, he was in a serious courtship with a young lady in his home country of England. He was serious in his intent to marry this young lady when God called him to serve the nation of China. When he shared his heart with her about this calling, she declined to join him overseas. Now at this point Hudson Taylor could have given up his call by God to go to China because of his love for this woman. But instead he sacrificed this relationship and went on to China. He left behind the woman he loved because he had heard the voice of God. He followed God's call, and he flowed with God's timing. Eventually he met and married Maria Dyer in China, and much was accomplished through their life together.

Although not very many of us are called to China, we want every one of our kids to love God so much that they will find it possible to be in sync with His timing, as well as hearing what He is calling them to do. Timing is such a big factor in discovering a sacred love story. Many times fifteen-year-olds have come to me to tell me that they have met "the one." Fine, but is it God's timing? They have several years (at least!) ahead of them before they can run off and get married. This person might be the right one, but it is not in

God's timing for them to get married just yet. Or, as is most often the case, this is not the one God intends for them to marry.

In every case when it comes to timing, we can know that God is good, and we can believe that He always has our best in mind. Many situations come to mind where God's timing worked out so much better than if I had tried to figure it out myself.

I often tell teens and twenty-somethings that when it comes to the Lord and His timing with relationships, nothing good is ever lost in God. Here is what I mean by this principle: If a relationship presents itself and you are unsure this is the one that God has for you, place it on hold. Give the relationship some time apart. Since nothing good is ever lost in God, if the relationship does not work out, God has something better in mind. Now I am not saying that we need to do this with every relationship that comes along, but if the situation comes to that, do not be afraid to let the relationship go. God will keep intact what He wants for you. The key to remember is to keep your eyes on the Lord and what He is calling you to, and He will direct your path.

There is a proverb that I go back to again and again. We learned it as a family in our family devotions, and I pray it often.

> Roll your works upon the Lord [commit
> and trust them wholly to Him; He will
> cause your thoughts to become agreeable
> to His will, and] so shall your plans be
> established and succeed.
>
> —PROVERBS 16:3, AMP

In any situation that I face, but especially with relationship decisions that will chart the course of our lives, this verse has become my prayer. I put whatever situation I am facing on God's shoulders. I trust that particular situation so wholly to Him that I will allow God to change my thinking to become agreeable to His will. I know that if my thinking is in line with what the Lord wants, my actions will be in line as well, and He will establish my future destiny. So often we demand our own way and then ask God to bless it. We need to be teaching our kids to surrender completely to God. The best way to teach our children this principle is for us to model it for them.

A lady I met one day at a conference shared a story with me about a good friend who was a young missionary in Russia. He had felt strongly called to that nation, and he had wondered how he would ever meet a wife who would share the same heart and calling. After he had been there for a time, God placed it on his heart to return to the United States and earn his master's degree in theology. The day before he left Russia, the mission organization that he worked with had an all-staff meeting. There sitting across the table from him was a beautiful young lady. His heart leapt a bit that there was a single young lady working in Russia as he was, but he was leaving for two years the very next day! He figured it was not worth pursuing at that time, and he basically went on with his life. During seminary he thought of this woman regularly and could not get her out of his mind. He wondered if he would ever see her again.

After finishing his master's, he went back to Russia. On the first day after he returned, he was in the huge open market in Moscow getting some necessities. What should happen but that he looked up and there standing across from him was the woman he had met two years before! What are the chances of that happening? That had to be a "God setup" for sure. Well, they ended up getting married.

## ACCOUNTABILITY

The next basic guideline for a healthy sacred love story is accountability. A couple in a relationship needs to have someone whom they trust to give them perspective and to speak into the relationship. Ideally that should be Mom and Dad. Now this is not about controlling the relationship or riding around in the backseat of the car whenever the couple goes somewhere; your primary role is providing healthy perspective. Remember, our kids have to make their own choices when it comes to the one they are going to marry. Among other things, I certainly don't want to create a victim mentality in my child by picking his or her spouse, because then when the going gets tough, the blame will be directed toward me.

To achieve accountability, you must have proximity. Sometimes our young adult children do not live near us anymore. They might be away at college or have taken a job in another state. It is important that they find someone to whom they can be accountable in that area. It might be a local church pastor and spouse or long-time family friends, someone who will check in on the relationship. Even if we live far away from our kids and it is possible to keep tabs with technology, they also need someone who is nearby.

What does accountability look like when your kids are pursuing their sacred love story? You need to be asking them what God is speaking to them about the direction of the relationship. This happens before they ever even come together as a couple. This is a place where Dad's role as a protector is important. Especially when our kids are younger and in their teen years, having relationship inquiries go through Dad is significant. One time I met a lady who said that her husband gave their daughter business cards with his name and number on it. He instructed her that if a guy asks for her phone number to ask her out, to give him that card and have him call him first.

Don't think just because you have a son that the he will do all the asking. No, in our world today we have to protect our sons as well. Girls these days have no limits in pursuing boys. Your son might be only twelve, but get ready for the calls to start rolling in. It's essential to have some boundaries in place for him too.

Accountability is important with physical boundaries. Somebody needs to be asking the couple how their standard is holding up. Somebody might need to help them set parameters on being alone together to help them stay pure.

So many relationships in our world today have an unhealthy foundation. Some relationships exist solely to serve the purpose of idolizing the other person. This fuels the inborn desire for worship, and it can cascade into a worship program that looks something like this: "I will worship you if you worship me and the very ground I walk on." This is not a healthy way to start a relationship. True worship belongs to God alone, and the more we take it for ourselves, the more entrenched iniquity will become in our lives. Our one true desire needs to be toward God and any relationship that complements our worship of Him. So many young people are looking for a person to fulfill their desire for intimacy, when it is God alone who is capable of doing that.

We as parents need to hold our young people accountable when it comes to these and other unhealthy patterns. Not only will these patterns not disappear when they get married, but they will also sabotage their married life.

Addictive relationship patterns are also something to be aware of. Addictive and controlling relationships are steeped in possessiveness, and an addictive person will not be able to function with anyone outside the relationship itself. If you notice an extreme exclusivity, the warning lights should be flashing. Often it is difficult for those who are immersed in these unhealthy patterns to identify them, which makes it even more vital to have a system for accountability that can alert the couple to the destructive patterns that they exhibit.

## SPIRITUAL AND EMOTIONAL BOUNDARIES

Lastly, couples need boundaries that are not only physical but spiritual and emotional as well. The growth of a relationship needs to be in sync with the depth of commitment. As Dr. Don Raunikar outlines in his book, *Choosing God's Best*, this is part of the whole problem with our modern approach to romantic relationships. Our culture's practice of dating disrupts the God-orchestrated commitment level that we need to reach before the physical relationship starts. Otherwise, he writes:

> When the physical, emotional or spiritual level of involvement is greater than the commitment level, [you experience] counterfeit oneness....Dating emphasizes emotions, lust, and sensual desire—all of which demand a sexual response....Even singles who don't want to become physically involved often do because they are fighting the very natures God gave them.[2]

When a couple does not have a solid commitment to a sacred love story, this is not the time to be revealing deep, emotional, heartfelt issues or praying one-on-one together. Oftentimes this is how young people, especially teens, become attracted to someone out of sync with God's plan. Sharing deep feelings and delving into deep spiritual discussions about future hopes and dreams will only generate feelings of closeness and desire. As this sharing achieves depth in the spiritual and emotional realm, a corresponding physical realm cries out for depth as well. In other words, when couples pursue the spiritual and emotional levels, then the physical will inevitably follow. This is the way God has designed us. If our young people have an understanding of this, they can save this depth of sharing for when it is the right timing and they have heard from God that this is the one they are to marry—their sacred love story. Then the relationship can grow in depth on every level (while still maintaining clear physical boundaries) as the depth of commitment is increased.

Keep in mind that a sacred love story from God is creatively crafted by the hand of the master architect Himself. Each of our children, if they are open to the master's hand, will eventually pursue the exciting journey of letting Him create their life's design.

# Chapter 12

# PROJECT BLESSING

As our kids grow up in the midst of the hostile culture in which God has placed our families, they face enormous opposition to achieving pure lives and well-balanced personalities. They need solid assurance that not only do we as their parents stand behind them, but also that God Himself is backing them up 100 percent. This assurance comes through intentional parental *blessings*. The language of blessing provides a way to speak truth and vision into our children's lives, which will undergird them in every way.

Most of us parents were never blessed while we were growing up. I mean our parents might have communicated their love for us, but they never communicated a spiritual blessing from God the Father to us. A blessing is like a mantle being passed from the throne of heaven and placed on our shoulders. Since we lacked this blessing, many of us have been searching for it our entire lives. We have looked high and low for affirmation, someone to pat us on the back saying, "I love you. You are blessed. You are worthy. You do a fantastic job." We have tried to achieve this through grades, jobs, relationships, and other means. Because God's unconditional blessing was never communicated to us through our parents, we naturally thought we had to earn it.

Meanwhile, all along our Father in heaven has been loving us unconditionally—He is pleased with us. God alone is the one who can give this affirmation and love we seek, and God can use us as parents to help our kids find this love and acceptance by blessing them.

## "I LOVE YOU"

I want to give you an example of blessing and the power of our words over our children. The following story is from my husband, Kay, who grew up in California in a traditional Japanese-American household.

"I love you!" Three very powerful words. Three words that have a huge impact on you. I can count on my hand the number of times my father said, "I love you," to me. As a father now, I look back and see how those times shaped me into who I was and am today. There is power in words, but these three have a supernatural power to bless.

The first time my father said he loved me was when I was named Outstanding Boy in my junior high school at the age of thirteen. To put this in context, I was very shy and introverted until twelve. In seventh grade a teacher shared with me that I had potential and a destiny. How could he say this to me? I was not athletic, nor very popular. I was the only minority in the school, reading books during the recess, and I had glasses with braces too! But those words, *destiny* and *potential*, really sparked in me a motivation to change.

With his encouragement and help, I studied successful political campaigns and became the president of Pioneer Jr. High School. After a year serving as president, playing in the band, starting to run track and excelling in my studies, the school gave me the award at graduation. From a meek, Japanese American introvert at twelve, I was now a "cool" leader wearing Hang Ten shirts and K-Swiss shoes. But what I really wanted to know was whether my dad loved me.

I can still remember it like it was yesterday. It was a hot, sunny day in Upland, California. At the end of graduation and the presentation of the award by the principal, our family went to the front of the auditorium to take a picture. As I stood there with my father and mother on each side, me in my new dark blue, three-piece suit that my mother just bought for me, my dad turns and says to me, "Son, I am proud of you. I love you." With those words I associated that my performance in school and bringing honor to the family was directly related to his love. I was set! For the last twelve years I had been looking for his love and affirmation and now I had the key to his heart. In high school I was an honors student, cross-country runner, class president, and vice president of the high school. I filled my days and nights with activities, but always it was never enough it seemed. On the weekends and summers I would work for my dad, who had a landscaping and gardening business. I would out-perform and push myself more than the Mexican and Honduran workers in the 105 degree heat, carrying more loads of rubbish and cutting lawns faster and better than the next man. In all this I was looking for a kind word of affirmation from my dad.

It was not until I found Jesus Christ, or rather more accurately Jesus Christ found me, that I found my true identity as a man. When God tells you that He loves you, there is both a freeing and a captivating aspect to those words. It is freeing in that you can now be all that God has called you to become and destined to be! You are free to be as He made you and called you into existence to be, no matter what your life has been like. He frees you from the guilt, pain, lack, and shame of the past! He launches you to an exciting life of endless possibilities with a supernat-ural God! In this love relationship with God, there is a captivating part that makes us His bondservant.

Forever, we become His servant to do His will here on earth. His love enfolds us in His arms, and we struggle in our flesh to become comfortable in His will for our lives. In this grasp, our flesh or inner man dies to its desires and iniquity and then transforms into His likeness and character. We become love to the world, reflecting His love to those we touch, speak to, and love.[1]

## PROJECT BLESSING

We have done something in our family for years now that we call Project Blessing. Our kids have come to love it so much that they run to our sides whenever Kay says that he is going to initiate our family's Project Blessing.

We have the opportunity to express the love of God to our children. It is very simple, yet has a powerfully far-reaching impact. Especially for fathers who deeply desire to influence their children but so often have shared with me that they feel ineffectual, Project Blessing will plant seeds that will return a great harvest in their children's lives.

Our family often takes the opportunity to do Project Blessing when Kay is going out of town on business and will be gone for several days. Many families might incorporate this into their Sunday activities as part of their family's worship time. I know that others do this on their child's birthday.

It is great to bless your family on a regular and consistent basis. Whether weekly or monthly, Project Blessing will fill your children with a tremendous sense of God the Father looking down and smiling on them with His zealous heart of love for them.

> *In many cultures people go their entire lives without hearing the words "I love you" from their parents.*

When we call our kids to our side, my husband prays for each child from the youngest to the oldest. He makes sure that he lays his hands on each of them as he prays for them. When he gets on one knee, looks each of them in the eye, holds them, and says the blessing, there is a connection that goes far beyond words. An emotional and spiritual blessing takes place.

He usually begins each child's prayer by telling her specifically that he loves her. This is a powerful component. Many of us take for granted that telling our children verbally that we love them is an acceptable, everyday practice, but as I have ministered around the world, I have learned that in many cultures this is not normal. In many cultures people go their entire lives without hearing the words "I love you" from their parents. Parents both here in Western nations and in nations tucked into the farthest corners of the earth have told me that they do not know how to express "I love you" to their children.

When we bless our family, we look each child in the eyes and simply say, "I love you." Even if you never heard these words from your parents or did not hear them frequently enough, don't let the enemy rob you of the opportunity to bless your own children. This is important for you to do even if this is new territory for you and you have never ventured here before.

When I have witnessed dads, especially, saying these exact words for the first time to their kids, let me tell you, this is an incredibly powerful moment to witness. When these words come from a sincere heart and flow into a young man or woman for the first time, years of walls that have been built up between generations melt away. I have seen God powerfully use this with little ones as well as adult children. God's spirit comes, and a supernatural healing of wounds occurs. This is not just the statement of love coming from the mom or dad; it is the river of God's tremendous love that covers a multitude of sin flowing from His throne through parents that He is using as vessels to pour into the next generation.

Another element we include in our family's blessing time is to point out the unique gifts and callings that God has given each child. We speak into their lives, calling out how God may use that gift in the future. For example, Kay might pray over our daughter Hana like this, "God, I thank You that Hana has such a love for Your Word and that You are going to raise her up to be a mighty woman of God who will tell others about the power in Your Word."

We also affirm an area in their lives where we see that God has been at work forming their character and actions into His likeness. Picking a specific area where God has been transforming them encourages them to see that the Lord is at work in their lives. Kay might continue to pray in this direction, "Hana, you have been such an amazing helper to your mom this week, and you have especially helped by getting along with your little sister, Mikayla. God is so pleased with your effort and choices to be such a good-hearted big sister."

We want to spotlight an area where we see improvement in our child's actions and character. It might be that this child worked on getting homework in on time. Maybe this week the other child was especially helpful and dutiful with chores that had previously presented a struggle. Sometimes we parents have such a critical eye toward our children. When we are constantly critical, our kids get the impression that we feel they are never quite up to snuff. This is an opportunity for us to work on seeing where they are improving and where God is at work in their lives and to affirm that. This is how the blessings of God can flow through Mom and Dad and be transferred into our children's lives.

When I studied biblical blessings, looking at especially Abraham, Isaac, and Jacob, I was impacted by the way God's blessing communicates how much He loves us and is pleased with us. Blessings communicate literal healing and financial provision. Blessings emphasize the mantle and call of God to every generation. Blessings represent a place where God smiles on us. I believe that if our generation knew the depth of how God smiles on us and loves us so abundantly, we would approach the throne of God—and life—very differently. The assurance that "God is good all the time" would resound in us instead of making doubt weigh heavily upon us.

This is why we want to make time for Project Blessing in our homes. We want our kids, from a young age as exemplified through us as their parents, to have such an understanding of the goodness of God and how He has their best in mind.

In our family Kay is the one who primarily prays our family's blessing. At times I pray as well for each one of them. In your family if Dad is willing and available to pray the blessing, this is wonderful. When Dad's plate is full of commitments and his schedule is tied down because of work, this is such a straightforward and uncomplicated way for him to have an enormous impact on his family. It is something that takes but a few minutes, yet the fruit of these blessing times will last a lifetime in your child.

Hopefully Project Blessing is something that will be carried on for generations in your family line. Initiating Project Blessing is a powerful way to break the family curses that have dwelt in family lines for generations.

Now if you are in a situation where you are a single mom or your husband is not available, be it physically or emotionally, you can lead Project Blessing in your home. This is a wonderful opportunity for you to speak life over your children and give them vision for their future. The Holy Spirit can "stand in" for the missing spouse. You can intercede in the role of the parent and pray God's blessing for your family! The Lord knows what you are going through with your family, and He is more than able to equip you and give you the grace to pray blessings on the family. One of the lies of the enemy, the devil, is to tell you that you are less than a family because of a missing spouse or parent. The truth from heaven is that God is with you, that you are not alone and God will empower you with enough grace and love for two parents!

## PROJECT BLESSING PRAYER

I have included an example Project Blessing prayer that you can customize for your family. Be led by the Spirit as to how to pray for your own children.

> *Heavenly Father,*
>
> *I present to You this day my precious child, _____.*
>
> *Thank You for this gift that You have given our family.*
>
> *Father, I know You love _____ so much. I love you, my child.*
>
> *Thank You for the unique gifts and talents You have bestowed upon this child.*
>
> *It is a blessing to see _____ walk in the fruit of Your Spirit and in the light of Your love.*
>
> *Thank You for the calling and destiny that You have in store for my child.*
>
> *You have an amazing plan and future for his/her life.*
>
> *I commit _____ to You, Father, and we ask that You would lead and guide this child in Your ways.*
>
> *Lord, we invite You to mold, shape, and disciple _____ to be the instrument that You have designed him/her to be.*

*I thank You for this time of preparation, and how I see my child growing in mind, heart, and body.*

*I am honored to be _____'s parent.*

*I know that You will never leave or forsake _____.*

*You are my child, a joy and a blessing.*

*May you fulfill all that God has in store for you.*

*May you be a mighty child of the living God who serves, loves, and obeys the Lord always.*

*In Jesus's name, amen.*

## STANDING AGAINST THE TIDE

God desires to pour out His Spirit and anoint our families to stand up for Him and His ways in a world that is crumbling. We cannot expect to do this in our own strength. We need to communicate to our children that to stand strong in a world of darkness is not something that we are able to accomplish in and of ourselves. The power of the Holy Spirit is necessary.

Parents, where this holy generation begins is with each child that God has placed into our families to raise up to follow the one true God. It is our job as guardians of purity to walk with them through the maze of choices in our culture so they can be more than conquerors.

We need to reiterate this message for the next generation: "Yet in all these things we are more than conquerors through Him who loved us" (Rom. 8:37). We want them to carry a mantle of purity of mind, heart, and body. I believe that God is searching for a holy generation that will light a fire of revival that will spread to the ends of the earth. I believe our children are of the holy generation that will unleash a holy fire that will turn the tide of culture back to God.

# NOTES

## Introduction
## Wake Up and Smell the Deception

1. Ann Oldenburg, "Sex and TV," *USA Today*, November 9, 2005, http://www.usatoday.com/life/television/news/2005-11-09-sex-on-tv_x.htm (accessed April 13, 2012).

2. Clean Cut Media, "Teens: Imitating 87 Hours of Watching Porn," April 20, 2009, www.cleancutmedia.com/article/teens-imitating-87-hours-of-watching-porn (accessed July 29, 2011).

3. The National Campaign to Prevent Teen Pregnancy, "Fast Facts: How Is the 3 in 10 Statistic Calculated?", http://www.thenationalcampaign.org/resources/pdf/FastFacts_3in10.pdf (accessed April 13, 2012).

4. Centers for Disease Control and Prevention, "Youth Risk Behavior Surveillance—2005," *Morbidity and Mortality Weekly Report* 55, no. SS-5 (June 9, 2006), http://www.cdc.gov/mmwr/pdf/ss/ss5505.pdf (accessed July 25, 2011).

5. The National Campaign to Prevent Teen and Unplanned Pregnancy, "That's What He Said: What Guys Think About Sex, Love, Contraception, and Relationships," http://www.thenationalcampaign.org/resources/pdf/pubs/ThatsWhatHeSaid.pdf (accessed October 17, 2011).

6. Ibid.

7. William Mosher, Anjani Chandra, and Jo Jones, "Sexual Behavior and Selected Health Measures: Men and Women 15–44 Years of Age, United States, 2002," *Advance Data From Vital and Health Statistics* 362 (September 15, 2005): 21–26.

8. Jerry Ropelato, "Internet Pornography Statistics," Best Internet Filter Software Review, http://www.internet-filter-review.toptenreviews.com/internet-pornography-statistics.html (accessed July 29, 2011).

9. Hillard Weinstock, Stuart Berman, and Willard Cates, Jr., "Sexually Transmitted Diseases Among American Youth:

Incidence and Prevalence Estimates," *Perspectives on Sexual and Reproductive Health* 36, no. 1 (January/February 2004): 6–10, as referenced at http://www.guttmacher.org/pubs/journals/3600604.html (accessed April 26, 2012).

10. Josh McDowell, *The Bare Facts: 39 Questions Your Parents Hope You Never Ask About Sex* (Chicago: Moody Publishers, 2011).

11. Kaiser Family Foundation, "Daily Media Use Among Children and Teens Up Dramatically From Five Years Ago," January 20, 2010, http://www.kff.org/entmedia/entmedia012010nr.cfm (accessed October 1, 2011).

12. Joe S. McIlhaney, Jr. and Freda McKissic Bush, *Hooked: New Science on How Casual Sex is Affecting Our Children* (Chicago: Moody Publishers, 2008), 57.

13. Lisa D. Lieberman, Heather Gray, Megan Wier, et al., "Long-Term Outcomes of an Abstinence-Based, Small-Group Pregnancy Prevention Program in New York City Schools," *Family Planning Perspectives* 32, no. 5 (September/October 2000), as referenced at http://www.guttmacher.org/pubs/journals/3223700.html (accessed April 26, 2012).

14. Kaiser Family Foundation, "Virginity and the First Time," October 2003, http://www.kff.org/entpartnerships/upload/Virginity-and-the-First-Time-Summary-of-Findings .pdf (accessed February 7, 2012).

15. Vincent Guilamo-Ramos, James Jaccard, Patricia Dittus, et al., "Parental Expertise, Trustworthiness, and Accessibility: Parent-Adolescent Communication and Adolescent Risk Behavior," *Journal of Marriage and Family* 68, no. 5 (December 2006): 1229–1246, as referenced at http://www.familyfacts.org/briefs/42/parents-influence-on-adolescents-sexual-behavior (accessed April 26, 2012).

16. Monica Longmore, Wendy Manning, Peggy Giordano, "Preadolescent Parenting Strategies and Teens' Dating and Sexual Initiation: A Longitudinal Analysis," *Journal of Marriage and Family* 63, no. 2 (2001): 322–335, as referenced at http://www.familyfacts.org/briefs/42/parents-influence-on-adolescents-sexual-behavior (accessed April 26, 2012).

17. Melina Bersamin, Michael Todd, Deborah A. Fisher, et al., "Parenting Practices and Adolescent Sexual Behavior: A Longitudinal Study," *Journal of Marriage and Family* 70, (February 2008): 97–112, as referenced at http://www.familyfacts .org/briefs/42/parents-influence-on-adolescents-sexual-behavior (accessed April 26, 2012).

18. Cheryl B. Aspy, S. K. Vesely, R. F. Oman, et al., "Parental Communication and Youth Sexual Behavior," *Journal of Adolescence* 30, no. 3 (2007): 449–466, as referenced at http:// www.familyfacts.org/briefs/42/parents-influence-on- adolescents-sexual-behavior (accessed April 26, 2012).

19. Christian Smith and Melinda Lundquist Denton, *Soul Searching: The Religious and Spiritual Lives of American Teenagers* (London: Oxford University Press, 2005), 28.

## CHAPTER 1
## THE EVER-CHANGING LANDSCAPE OF TECHNOLOGY

1. The concept of Digital Natives and Digital Immigrants is taken from "Digital Natives, Digital Immigrants" by Marc Prensky *On the Horizon* (MCB University Press, Vol. 9 No. 5, October 2001), http://tinyurl.com/c8pfx55 (accessed April 26, 2012).

2. Karl Fisch, Scott McLeod, and Jeff Brenman, "Did You Know? 3.0," YouTube.com, http://www.youtube.com/ watch?v=jp_oyHY5bug&feature=related (accessed April 16, 2012).

3. The National Campaign to Prevent Teen and Unplanned Pregnancy, "Sex and Tech," 2008, http://www.thenational campaign.org/sextech/PDF/SexTech_Summary.pdf (accessed July 29, 2011).

4. Ibid.

5. Ropelato, "Internet Pornography Statistics."

6. Ibid.

7. Ron Luce, *Re-Create: Building a Culture in Your Home Stronger Than the Culture Deceiving Your Kids* (Ventura, CA: Gospel Light, 2011), 25.

8. Ropelato, "Internet Pornography Statistics."

9. Kaiser Family Foundation, "Daily Media Use Among Children and Teens Up Dramatically From Five Years Ago."

10. Ibid.

11. Enough Is Enough, "Pornography Statistics," http://www.internetsafety101.org/Pornographystatistics.htm (accessed July 27, 2011).

12. Ibid.

13. The National Campaign to Prevent Teen and Unplanned Pregnancy, "That's What He Said: What Guys Think About Sex, Love, Contraception, and Relationships."

14. Ralph Earle and Ken Wells, "Pastors and Porn," *Rev! Magazine*, July/August 2007, 52–55, http://www.rev.org/ArticlePrint.asp?ID=2514 (accessed October 1, 2011).

15. "One in Five Kids Has Been Propositioned for Cybersex," Legal Facts 2, no. 3, 2000.

16. Family Safe Media, "Children Internet Pornography Statistics," http://familysafemedia.com/pornography_statistics.html#anchor5 (accessed June 5, 2012).

17. Fred Stoeker and Jasen Stoeker, *Hero: Becoming the Man She Desires* (Colorado Springs, CO: Waterbrook Press, 2009), xiv.

18. Ropelato, "Internet Pornography Statistics."

## CHAPTER 2
## HOLLYWOOD HANGOVER

1. Victoria J. Rideout, Ulla G. Foehr, Donald F. Roberts, "Generation M$^2$: Media in the Lives of 8- to 18-Year-Olds," Kaiser Family Foundation, January 2010, http://www.kff.org/entmedia/upload/8010.pdf (accessed July 29, 2011).

2. Ibid.

3. Ibid.

4. Victoria J. Rideout, Elizabeth A. Vandewater, Ellen A. Wartella, "Zero to Six: Electronic Media in the Lives of Infants, Toddlers and Preschoolers," Kaiser Family Foundation, Fall 2003, http://www.kff.org/entmedia/loader.cfm?url=/

commonspot/security/getfile.cfm&PageID=22754 (accessed July 29, 2011).

5.  Kaiser Family Foundation, *The Media Family: Media in the Lives of Infants, Toddlers, Preschoolers, and their Parents*, May 2006.

6.  Ted Baehr, *The Media-Wise Family* (n.p: Media-Wise Publishing, 2005).

7.  Anita Chandra, Steven C. Martino, Rebecca L. Collins, et al., "Does Watching Sex on Television Predict Teen Pregnancy?" *Pediatrics* 122, no. 5 (November 1, 2008): 1047–1054, http://pediatrics.aappublications.org/content/122/5/1047.full .html (accessed October 1, 2011).

8.  Julie Hiramine, *Culture Shock: A Survival Guide for Teens* (Cincinnati, OH: Standard Publishing, 2011), 41.

## CHAPTER 3
## THE ROOTS OF FAMILY CONNECTEDNESS

1.  Society for Research in Child Development, as reported in ScienceDaily, "Fathers Respond to Teens' Risky Sexual Behavior With Increased Supervision," May 15, 2009, http://www.sciencedaily.com/releases/2009/05/090515083700.htm (accessed October 18, 2011).

2.  Vincent Guilamo-Ramos, James Jaccard, Patricia Dittus, Alida M. Bouris, "Parental Expertise, Trustworthiness, and Accessibility: Parent-Adolescent Communication and Adolescent Risk Behavior," *Journal of Marriage and Family* 68, no. 5 (December 2006): 1229–1246, as referenced at http://www .familyfacts.org/briefs/42/parents-influence-on-adolescents -sexual-behavior (accessed April 26, 2012). Carol A. Ford, Brian Wells Pence, William C. Miller, et al., "Predicting Adolescents' Longitudinal Risk for Sexually Transmitted Infection," Archives of Pediatric & Adolescent Medicine 159, (July 2005): 657–664, as referenced at http://www.familyfacts.org/briefs/42/ parents-influence-on-adolescents-sexual-behavior (accessed April 26, 2012).

3.  Josh McDowell and Dick Day, *How to Be a Hero to Your Kids* (Nashville: Thomas Nelson, 1993), 28.

4. Jane Mendle, K. Paige Harden, Eric Turkheimer, et al., "Associations Between Father Absence and Age of First Sexual Intercourse," *Child Development* 80, no. 5 (September-October 2009): 1463–1480. When you do the math presented in the study, it equals 250 percent.


## Chapter 4
## Patterns That Undermine Character

1. Amy LeFeuvre, retold by Mark Hamby, *Teddy's Button* (Waverly, PA: Lamplighter Publishing, 2005), 31.


## Chapter 5
## Parents: The Guardians of Purity

1. Julie Hiramine and Megan Briggs, *Against the Tide* (Colorado Springs, CO: Generations of Virtue, 2012).
2. Kris Vallotton and Jason Vallotton, *Moral Revolution: The Naked Truth About Sexual Purity* (Shippensburg, PA: Destiny Image Publishers, 2010), 93.


## Chapter 6
## Building Character That Lasts a Lifetime

1. Karen Santorum, *Everyday Graces* (Wilmington, DE: Intercollegiate Studies Institute, 2003).
2. We originally got the idea of "manners week" from Dennis and Barbara Rainey, who talk about it on their radio program, *FamilyLife Today*.


## Chapter 7
## Developing Purity Muscles

1. Timothy S. Grall, "Custodial Mothers and Fathers and Their Child Support: 2007," U.S. Census Bureau, Current Population Reports (November 2009), http://www.census .gov/prod/2009pubs/p60-237.pdf (accessed October 1, 2011).

2. Dannah Gresh, *Secret Keeper: The Delicate Power of Modesty* (Chicago: Moody, 2011).

## CHAPTER 8
## TALKING ABOUT THE BIRDS AND THE BEES

1. Larry Christenson, *The Wonderful Way Babies Are Made* (Grand Rapids, MI: Bethany House Publishers, 1982).

2. Jon Holsten, *The Swimsuit Lesson* (Fort Collins, CO: Holsten Books, 2009), 22.

3. American Psychological Association, "Child Sexual Abuse: What Parents Should Know," http://www.apa.org/pi/families/resources/child-sexual-abuse.aspx# (accessed April 24, 2012); Children's Center for Hope and Healing, "Protecting Our Children: Beyond 'Stranger Danger'," http://www.hopeandhealingga.org/pdf/beyondsdanger.pdf (accessed April 24, 2012).

4. Dennis and Barbara Rainey, *Beyond Abstinence: Helping Your Teen Stay Pure* (Little Rock, AR: FamilyLife Publishing, 1997).

5. Walt Larimore, *Lintball Leo's Not-So-Stupid Questions About Your Body* (Grand Rapids, MI: Zonderkidz, 2003), 16.

6. Alan Mozes, "Study Tracks Masturbation Trends Among U.S. Teens" HealthDay, August 1, 2011, http://health.usnews.com/health-news/family-health/womens-health/articles/2011/08/01/study-tracks-masturbation-trends-among-us-teens (accessed May 25, 2012).

7. Ibid.

8. Dennis and Barbara Rainey, *Passport2Purity* (Little Rock, AR: FamilyLife Publishing, 2012).

## CHAPTER 10
## THE DATING GAME

1. Jennie Bishop, *The Princess and the Kiss* (Anderson, IN: Warner Press, 2000).

2. Physiciansforlife.org titled "Cohabitation vs. Marriage: 26 Research Findings," compiled from The National Marriage Project, http://www.physiciansforlife.org/content/view/242/27/ (accessed February 16, 2012).

3. Josh McDowell and Bill Jones, *The Teenage Q & A Book* (Nashville: Thomas Nelson, 1990), 133.

4. Joe S. McIlhaney, Jr. and Freda McKissic Bush, *Hooked: New Science on How Casual Sex Is Affecting Our Children* (Chicago: Moody, 2008).

5. Leslie Ludy, *Authentic Beauty* (Colorado Springs, CO: Multnomah, 2003), 87.

6. Eric and Leslie Ludy, *When God Writes Your Love Story* (Colorado Springs, CO: Multnomah Books, 2009).

## Chapter 11
## Pursuing a Sacred Love Story

1. Marty Friedman, "Marriage and Divorce Statistics," http://www.meninmarriage.com/article05.htm (accessed October 20, 2011).

2. Don Raunikar, *Choosing God's Best* (Colorado Springs, CO: Multnomah Books, 1998), 58–59.

## Chapter 12
## Project Blessing

1. Kay Hiramine, *Project Blessing* (Colorado Springs, CO: Generations of Virtue, 2012).

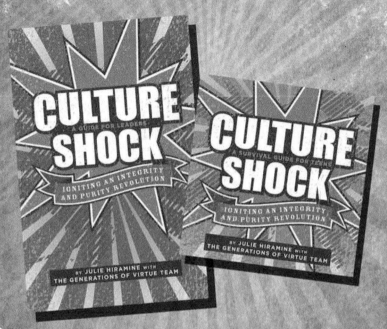

# raising a pure generation

## FOR PARENTS AND LEADERS

For parents of toddlers to teens, RAPG is an 8-session curriculum that trains parents in key areas of mentoring their children in purity. Parents will learn practical ways to connect with their children and equip them to choose God's love over the world's counterfeit.

Ideal for:
- Cell groups
- Moms groups
- Retreats
- Church leadership groups
- Bible studies
- Parenting Classes
- Couples date night/study
- Homeschool support groups

Complete with 4 DVDs, Leaders Guide, Parent's Guide, and access to bonus material and an interactive website.

generationsofvirtue.org/rapg